Gen Reimer,
    In appreciation for
your service for loyalty to
this great Nation & the US
military. A true Hero, I
personally salute your leadership,
& passion to answer the

NO GREATER LOVE

THE LIVES AND TIMES OF HISPANIC SOLDIERS

" call to duty." God Bless,
I remain Respectfully

Freddie Valenzuela

MAJOR GENERAL FREDDIE VALENZUELA, USA (RET.)

WITH JASON LEMONS, J.D.

Hooah!

OVATION
Books

No Greater Love: The Lives and Times of Hispanic Soldiers
Published by Ovation Books
P.O. Box 80107
Austin, TX 78758

For more information about our books, please write to us, call 512.478.2028, or visit our website at www.ovationbooks.net

Distributed to the trade by National Book Network, Inc.

Publisher's Cataloging-in-Publication
(Provided by Quality Books, Inc.)

    Valenzuela, Freddie.
       No greater love : the lives and times of Hispanic soldiers / Freddie Valenzuela ; with Jason Lemons.
       p. cm.
       Includes bibliographical references.
       LCCN 2007936487
       ISBN-13: 978-0-9790275-8-1
       ISBN-10: 0-9790275-8-6

       1. Valenzuela, Freddie. 2. United States. Army--Officers--Biography. 3. Generals--United States--Biography. 4. Hispanic American soldiers--Biography. 5. United States--Armed Forces--Hispanic Americans. I. Lemons, Jason. II. Title.

    U53.V34A3 2008   355'.0092
                   QBI08-600012

Front cover design by Priyanka Kodikal

Proceeds to benefit The General Alfred Valenzuela Family Foundation, an educational foundation for at-risk children and families of soldiers killed in the line of duty.

10 9 8 7 6 5 4 3 2

"Remember, remember always that all of us, and you and I especially, are descended from immigrants and revolutionists."

—President Franklin D. Roosevelt, remarks before the Daughters of the American Revolution, Washington, D.C., April 21, 1938.

DEDICATION

I write this story for all American soldiers, sailors, airmen, and marines, for it is their perseverance that allows the rest of us to enjoy the lives we lead. More specifically, I dedicate this book to the twenty-one soldiers who died defending this country in Iraq and Afghanistan and whose funerals I had the honor of presiding over. I also dedicate this book to the extraordinary families of these soldiers, whom I grieved with in the course of honoring their heroic children.

I never had the privilege of knowing these Hispanic-American heroes while they were alive, but their legacy is a great source of pride and inspiration for me. They were:

Pfc. Steven Acosta, Calexico, CA
Spc. Richard Arriaga, Ganado, TX
Spc. Robert R. Arsiaga, San Antonio, TX
Sgt. Michael Paul Barrera, Von Ormy, TX
Spc. Adolfo C. Carballo, Houston, TX
Spc. Zeferino E. Colunga, Bellville, TX
Pfc. Rey D. Cuervo, Laguna Vista, TX
Spc. Israel Garza, Lubbock, TX
Spc. Rodrigo Gonzalez-Garza, San Antonio, TX
Pfc. Analaura Esparza Gutierrez, Houston, TX
Pfc. Pablo Manzano, Heber, CA
Sgt. Gerardo Moreno, Terrell, TX*

Spc. Jose A. Perez III, San Diego, TX
Staff Sgt. Hector R. Perez, Corpus Christi, TX
Sgt. Juan M. Serrano, Manati, PR*
Pfc. Armando Soriano, Houston, TX
Cpl. Tomas Sotelo Jr., Houston, TX
Spc. Ramon Reyes Torres, Caguas, PR*
Sgt. Melissa Valles, Eagle Pass, TX
Chief Warrant Officer 2 Lawrence S. (Shane) Colton, Oklahoma City, OK
Spc. Tracy L. Laramore, Okaloosa, FL

May the memories of these twenty-one soldiers live on in our hearts and continue to inspire all Americans.

*I presided over these funerals in conjunction with other officers.

TABLE OF CONTENTS

FOREWORD

On his thirty-second birthday, Captain Alfred Valenzuela, "Freddie" to all of his friends, received a copy of General Omar Bradley's *A Soldier's Story* as a gift. The autobiography of the respected and beloved "GI General" seemed to be a perfect guide for this young officer who had earned his master's degree at St. Mary's University and was off to his next duty assignment. As one of Freddie's university professors and friends, I knew that he already had the motivation, discipline, and leadership qualities to succeed in the army. I did not foresee at that time, however, the heights to which his leadership abilities, his love of family and of the army, and his care and compassion for others would take him.

Both General Omar Bradley and Major General Alfred Valenzuela benefited in early childhood from strong and supportive families. The conditions of early life for Freddie on San Antonio's west side and Bradley's childhood in rural Missouri were environments that challenged and taught both men the need for education and the priceless value of enduring friendships. Freddie's parents worked hard to ensure their children's success in education and later in careers. To this day, Sarah and Alfred Valenzuela remain attentive, solid pillars for the ever-increasing Valenzuela family of grandchildren and great grandchildren. An indelible experience of the enduringly strong bonds of family became the chief source of Freddie's dedication, care, and compassion throughout his army career and beyond.

No Greater Love depicts fully the centrality of family life in the military. Freddie attests to the proposition that "every soldier I have known will confirm that their family remains the most cherished element in their complicated life." He will quickly tell anyone he encounters that the sacrifices made by his own wife and children while in the military were what allowed him to be so successful in an arena rarely entered by Hispanic soldiers. The wisdom of family solidarity and support contained in this book has great contemporary relevance. A unique feature of *No Greater Love* is the family's story told in their own words by wife, daughter, and son—Esther, Lori, and Freddie Junior. Esther affirms the importance of family unity amid a career that calls for dozens of moves and duty assignments: "I believe that my husband's and our family's [successes] came about because we never lost sight of each other. The army was the roadmap of our lives, but we never forgot who was in the vehicle." There could be no better roadmap for today's military families than the affirmation of unity found in these stories.

One of the most poignant accounts in *No Greater Love* is the transformation in Freddie's life as a result of taking part in the burials of twenty-one soldiers who sacrificed their lives for their country. Family loss, sacrifice, patriotism, and the stature of heroes combine to give meaning and purpose to Freddie's thirty-three year career in the United States Army. In spending time with grieving mothers and fathers, in summarizing acts of bravery and heroism, Freddie found the motivation and purpose of this book. He is concerned throughout with the lives of soldiers and with the army life as a career.

To that end, *No Greater Love* provides insight and understanding of the army as an institution, especially for Hispanic men and women. He counsels, but never condemns. He encourages and commends Hispanic service achievements, but never at the expense of the institution that he cherishes or the culture that nurtured him. Rather, he challenges a profession and an institution that he loves to become better. He also shows the way to an engaged life of service after retirement from the army.

Holding steadfast to the discipline, focus, and drive he learned in the army, Freddie Valenzuela moved back to San Antonio after retiring as commanding general of the U.S. Army South. He wasted no time in giving his significant energy and experience to improving education for children and university students by immediately laying the groundwork for an educational foundation. Two groups of youngsters are recipients of the foundation's good works. First are the students who attend his charter school, the General Alfred A. Valenzuela Intermediate Leadership Academy, which serves children in grades six through eight. The location of the academy is very intentional; it proudly stands in San Antonio's west side, where educational success is vital and the inspiration of successful Hispanic role models is sorely needed. The second group, family members of fallen Hispanic soldiers, benefit from scholarships awarded by the foundation.

Freddie also gives freely of his time and expertise to his alma mater, St. Mary's University, where he served as an officer on the board of trustees. He has continued an exhaustive schedule of motivational speaking to youth in San Antonio and throughout the nation. He undertakes all efforts with the same enthusiasm and care that he exercised as a general officer in the army. He has successfully transitioned from the soldier's soldier to the citizen's citizen. We who know him believe that this new career is just beginning.

The reader should know that a significant portion of the proceeds from *No Greater Love* will go toward Freddie's educational foundation and the families of the twenty-one soldiers he has helped lay to rest. I believe that through his actions, and through the stories herein, you will come to know—as I have—the great and ongoing love affair that Freddie has with his country and with improving the lives of children through education. You will also come to understand that everything Freddie does, he does for the future of this nation.

Charles Cotrell
President
St. Mary's University
October 2007

PREFACE

You may wonder why I decided to write this book. Am I writing my story for fame and glory? For the money or to satisfy my ego? In all sincerity, I did not write this book for purposes of self-aggrandizement. In fact, the one thing I knew for certain when I began writing this book was that I didn't want it to be about me. The last thing I want to be accused of is vanity. For the longest time, I have resisted the urge to tell my story, but as I explored and researched the legacy of Hispanic Americans in the military, I soon learned that the best way I could tell the story of our amazing Hispanic military men and women was to take the time to tell my own. Their story is my story—a shared experience. Thus, my ultimate goal is to articulate a history that others have neglected to document.

But this book is not meant to be a mere history of Hispanics in the military; in many ways, I want to help today's Hispanic servicemen and women prepare for their own journey and legacy in our armed forces. Furthermore, I feel it is important that the family members of these soldiers know and understand exactly the things expected of their loved ones who have assumed the burden of sacrifice and for whom we are absolutely grateful.

The first part of the title for my book comes from the bible verse in John 15:13: "Greater love hath no man than this, that a man lay down his life for his friends." These words describe exactly what servicemen and women have done for their country time and time again. Some of these heroes didn't even consider the gravity of the things they did at the time; they simply did it for the benefit of their country and for their brothers and sisters on the battlefield.

The name of my book also provides direction for the General Alfred Valenzuela Family Foundation, the educational foundation I started for at-risk children. The proceeds for the sale of the book will benefit my foundation as well as the children of the families of the soldiers whom I had the honor of burying. I hope that this tribute will be remembered in the future of the United States Army's history. To our fallen comrades who faithfully answered the call of duty and paid the ultimate sacrifice, there truly is no greater love in existence.

The second part of the title—*The Lives and Times of Hispanic Soldiers*—emphasizes the character of Hispanic servicemen and women, their sacrifices over the last 232 years, and the challenges that they face as members of our great armed forces. I really cannot say enough about these patriots and the role they play in protecting our nation and its freedoms. In short, Hispanic soldiers, sailors, airmen, and marines performed heroically in times of war and peace without ever asking for anything special for their service. They answered their country's calling when drafted, and many others volunteered to serve, because they felt compelled to do their part to protect this nation and ensure its prosperity.

As I write this preface in February of 2007, our nation grapples with a growing number of serious issues, including progress in the Iraq War, our unpredictable economy, our need to improve access for all children to a quality education, our efforts to prepare preemptively for a possible pandemic outbreak, and our need to improve preparedness at all levels of government for future natural disasters. In spite of all of these contentious topics, immigration continues to take center stage in our ongoing national debate. Clearly, many Americans look across our southern border with fear and trepidation. Some of these fears are understandable, but many of them are borne of ignorance. U.S. Hispanics must reassure these Americans that we share their hopes and aspirations for this nation. Moreover, we must remind all Americans of the attributes that Hispanics bring to the proverbial "melting pot" every day. Toward that end, this book articulates the unique perspective of those of us who count ourselves as Americans first, Hispanics second, and it depicts the value that Hispanics contribute to the U.S. military in the face of the challenges that many of them confront due to their non-citizenship.

Every American should know the stories of these patriotic service-men and women. Those serving today want to take part in the American dream; moreover, they want to manifest their love for their country (or their adopted country). This love affair with our nation defies description and is most obvious in the stories of the forty-two Hispanic soldiers who were awarded the Congressional Medal of Honor.

Although some of these heroes were born in other countries, such as Spain, Chile, and Mexico, they gave of themselves with such valor and hero-ism as to cause Americans to marvel at their patriotism and selflessness. Four of the medal recipients were noncitizens of the United States at the time of their swearing in to the U.S. military, and many people I have worked with suspect that over one half of current Congressional Medal of Honor recipients could claim some type of immigrant status at the time they were honored. These men and women make their mark and sometimes give their lives for us without regard to their country of birth. However, many of them are forgotten when the time comes to honor them, and the lack of fanfare that we dedicate to their legacy is often deafening.

An additional goal in writing this book, therefore, was to try to make the playing field more level and to help the army become more sensitive to diversity issues and stave off any backlash based on ill perceptions. Honestly, I think the army's promotion and award system is objectively fair, but it is still important that we learn to document when needed and push the enve-lope toward inclusiveness, especially when recognizing deserving soldiers. Too often, the bureaucracy gets the best of us, and we allow ourselves to settle for the easier path rather than challenging the army to do the right thing in recognizing all deserving soldiers.

Our nation has placed an enormous burden upon its armed forces. We have asked them to be both warriors and statesmen in times of great uncer-tainty. We've trained our soldiers as lethal combatants prepared for risky situations while also asking them to be our moral conscience, unwavering in the face of the complex ethical, legal, and moral situations that the War on Terror places them in. Too often, this burden has been placed upon our servicemen and women with only limited guidance.

However, the history of this military institution suggests that if any-one can pull off the difficult task of bearing our country's liability, it is our soldiers. I pray I have provided valuable additional guidance in preparing others for the upcoming challenges on the horizon, which will be unlike any that our military has faced in the past. Hopefully, this book portrays our warriors as more than simple servicemen and women; after all, most of them end up playing the diverse and difficult roles of diplomat, peacekeeper, negotiator, missionary, mentor, role model, and nation builder. The U.S. Army attempts to accomplish its mission, and there should be no doubt that our soldiers can stand up to meet the challenges yet to come.

More than twenty years prior to our nation's bloody Civil War, Ralph Waldo Emerson contemplated on the role of the war and peace and its effect on humanity as a whole. Contrary to prevailing conventional wisdom, he argued that "war educates the senses, calls into action the will, perfects the physical constitution, brings men into such swift and close collision in critical moments that man measures man. On its own scale, on the virtues it loves, it endures no counterfeit, but shakes the whole society, until every atom falls into the place its specific gravity assigns it." Emerson understood that war, despite its tragic brutality, was often the catalyst that shaped the character of the men and women who experienced it. But its impact echoed beyond the lives of these individuals and actually shook and forever shaped the society and institutions that these soldiers fought to protect.

Unlike the American Civil War or even the ongoing fighting between Israel and Islam, our current war in Iraq rarely shakes the foundations of our modern society. Americans are still able to go on with their lives without enduring the fear and hardship that accompany war. But the War on Terror still is capable of shocking us on occasion. Today, our Internet-fueled media never sleeps, and it often shoves its way into the national consciousness when some round number of casualties is reached in our current conflict. However, in a nation of three hundred million people, the physical, financial, and mortal burden of the War on Terror is borne by an exceedingly small number of proud American families. These are the families who I came to know and respect when I buried twenty-one of their loved ones. They deserve our honor for raising these heroes from the ground up; moreover, they deserve our eternal gratitude for their sacrifice in our name. As we continue on in our War on Terror, we must never forget the sacrifices of these special soldiers. And we should never forget that there is another army of unadorned, overlooked families who also gave our country an invaluable gift in the men and women they raised.

My vision for this book is to help our current generation pave the way for their own time-honored legacy. These words tell an important story of whom these men and women really are, what great things they have done in the past, and why future generations will continue to repeat these acts of bravery and compassion in the future. This book is about them, for them, and written in prose to help others understand our past and who we are today. It is written in the vernacular of the Hispanic culture to better help ensure that these heroes are recognized for their exceptional service. Simple, humble, direct, and deliberate, this book exists solely for the benefit of our current and future soldiers.

If I had a message to pass on to this generation of Hispanic veterans, it would be in the form of the following words attributed to an unknown author:

We must be content to live without watching ourselves live, to work without expecting an immediate reward, to love without instantaneous satisfaction, and to exist without special recognition.

My Hispanic brethren and other great Americans have fully understood why some must live this way; they understood that our incredible nation was built, in large part, by men and women who remain largely anonymous to most Americans. And the legacy of the soldiers I buried further demonstrates the truth of the passage. These men and women dedicated and ultimately gave their lives to protect our country and build a better world for their families and countrymen without taking time to worry about whether they would be recognized for their efforts.

Make no mistake—I am an American, first and foremost. In fact, I frequently describe myself to others as an American soldier who just happens to be of Hispanic heritage. When I think about my lineage, I'm often reminded of the statement President Clinton made when bestowing the Congressional Medal of Honor on Alfredo Rascon: "Thank you...for reminding us that being an American has nothing to do with the place of your birth, the color of your skin, the language of your parents, or the way you worship God." Not coincidentally, Alfredo Rascon was also born in Mexico and was only a resident, not a citizen, of the United States when he saved the lives of his comrades in the 173rd Airborne Brigade in Vietnam and when he was later awarded the Medal of Honor.

From Rascon's example, we can see how strongly Hispanic-American soldiers feel for their country, or adopted country, and for soldiering. I personally define the Hispanic love affair with military service as conditional and unconditional in peace and in war. It is conditional in the sense of the tough love, discipline, and tireless work ethic required to succeed in service. But it is unconditional in that the call to military service is not done for benefit, luxury, or pecuniary gain, but rather for patriotism, love of country, service to others, and personal sacrifice. *No Greater Love* is about paying the ultimate price. With few exceptions, these excellent leaders are faceless and nameless except to their families, friends, and the fellow servicemen and women with whom they share the bond. Known only to God in some cases, I can help justify their heroism and shed light on whom they really are.

Although they served in a democratic fighting force, the soldiers profiled in this book emerged from what military historians refer to as the fog of war and proved to be worthy torch carriers of the uncommon aristocracy of valor. It has been said that a nation is defined by its heroes; if that's the case, this book was written to honor twenty-one of the greatest heroes our nation has ever known.

ACKNOWLEDGMENTS

As I remember and recognize the great people who have helped Esther and me along our path, I feel it necessary to say what their support meant to us during our journey. As I have stated in the book, if the U.S. Army is truly committed to promoting diversity within the institution, it must continue to increase minority representation in the ranks. This requires that senior leadership—starting with the administration and going all the way down through the military hierarchy—openly commit itself to the recruitment, retention, development, and support of those servicemen and service-women who were previously forgotten. Our leadership must educate and convince others that this initiative carries important strategic value and will help ensure the long-term vitality of the Institution. Thus, the secretary of defense and his service chiefs must recognize that the many opponents of our efforts are content to wait for the initiative to lose momentum, fall fur-ther down the list of priorities, and eventually die a natural death. Thus, all of us who believe that institutional diversity is vital to the long-term health of the army must remain vigilant and continue to persuade opponents and fence-sitters that our efforts are worthwhile.

No diversity initiative can sustain itself without great leadership and foresight from its proponents. The people I will mention below stand out as the true foot soldiers in this effort. They are the visionaries who understood the importance of diversity and its long-term benefit to the army we all love dearly. On behalf of myself and my family, I wish to thank the follow-ing folks who have served as mentors, alter egos, confidantes, believers and friends. These people all had a role in telling my story and the story of these extraordinary American soldiers of Hispanic heritage who left an indelible footprint on the history and evolution of our nation. Simply put, this book would never have been written without the support and encouragement of these people. I still take full responsibility for the content of this book, as well as any substantive errors that may be contained within.

I offer thanks:

To my family for their support and contributions toward what is arguably the most important thing I have done in my adult life. I'd be remiss if I didn't thank the family of Specialist Rodrigo Gonzalez, as well as the families of the twenty others who gave their lives for this country. I am inspired by their leadership and sacrifice every day. May their courage and heroism live forever in our memories.

To my immediate staff and to those who were instrumental in my later success, such as Lieutenant Colonel (retired) Tony and Diana Torres, Alfredo Najera, Majors Andy McClain, Paul Weyrauch, Jorge Arredondo, and Reggie Salazar, Colonel Rick Riera, Lieutenant Colonel (retired) Jeff Addicott, Sergeant First Class (retired) Robert Smith, Robert Daniels, Lieutenant Colonel Rick Ullian, and Tony Cerrillo. Colonel J.J. Garcia, Colonel (retired) Jim Malcolm, and Colonel Sara Martinez Pastoor showed me as doctors and soldiers that these two roles were not mutually exclusive, and they motivated me to strive for that human touch in my leadership efforts. I also thank Doug Sanders, Buddy Aleman, Uncle Sonny, and Albert Trevino—all sources of inspiration galore. A special thanks is accorded to Matias and Lena Fernandez, Jero and Mary Esteve, and their respective families, for helping to reinforce the meaning of God and family in my life. Esther and I sincerely appreciate them taking us in and sharing with us their spiritual and cultural upbringing.

To Maggie Rivas-Rodriguez for her U.S. Latino and Latina World War II Oral History, Virgil Fernandez for his fantastic book *Hispanic Military Heroes*, and Rudi Rodriguez for his masterful research and writing on our rich Tejano history and our past Hispanic brethren. These talented writers and academics motivated me to contribute my own portion of Hispanic-American history.

To a number of outstanding organizations who have valiantly carried the mantle for our troops through thick and thin. I have come to admire the Gold and Blue Star Mothers of America for the unwavering support they have shown for their sons and daughters on the battlefield. Originally formed during World War II, they simply pledge their support to all of our troops and unfailingly honor the memories of our fallen heroes. Their generosity and strength is a national treasure. In addition, I have been continually inspired by the former soldiers who make up the Alamo Airborne Silver Wings Association. Their loyalty to each other and the soldiers who follow personifies what it means to be a "soldier once… and young." All of these paratroopers answered their nation's call at its time of greatest need, bravely jumping out into the unknown. They remain immortal American heroes who still refuse to bow to defeat. These are the soldiers who made me what I am today; later, they made me proud to be a general officer representing them in this great army. Command Sergeant Major (retired) Ed and Hope Fernandez and Sergeant Major (retired) Benito Guerrero are just a couple of these warrior heroes who keep the flame of service burning. May we continue to meet at the DropZone, a place that rekindles that exact flame that we all came to revere. I will never forget the sacrifices of the following soldiers: Martinez, Chacon, Solano, Reyes, Rangel, Dominguez, Reyna, and many, many more. Each of these Hispanic veterans has played an important role in protecting the American dream by fully committing to fighting for their country in every airborne unit in the army inventory. They are the epitome of true soldiers.

To my fellow flag officers and their families, all of whom Esther and I owe the deepest gratitude. They provided invaluable mentorship when we needed it, and they remain lifelong friends. We check in on each other infrequently, but these brothers in arms remain in my heart everyday. To the Wards, Wilhelms, Berdys, Campbells, Dubiks, Honores, Sanchezes, and Magruders, as well as three special mentors, Dick Cavazos, Mark Cisneros and Josue Robles. We thank them all from the bottom of our hearts. This story is also dedicated to Brigadier General (retired) Bernardo "Bernie" Negrete, whose premature death saddens us all.

To my co-author Jason Lemons, J.D., who helped live my story—a true civilian hero who, by virtue of writing this book, became a true soldier, today and beyond.

To my World War II veteran dad and son who took the brunt of trying to figure me out on how to be a good son and father. I don't think I excelled at either role, but they understood and helped me realize that the toughest relationship is doable even if it comes late. Thanks for your patience and understanding. On the same lines, I would be remiss if I failed to thank my wonderful son-in-law Sean, grandson Hayden, and JoJo, the most magnificent thing to enter my son's life.

Most importantly, I thank the women in my life. To my mother Sara Valenzuela, who gave birth to me and never denied me her love and encouragement. As of this writing, she continues to guide me toward the right thing, despite the odds. To my sisters, Deborah Treviño and Claudia Valenzuela, who were always there when I needed them. Debbie, my deceased sister, gave so much of herself in taking care of my parents in the many years I was away from home, and I am indebted to her always. As for Claudia, now that we have reunited and live close enough to see each other more frequently, I always look forward to the times we spend making up for lost time.

To my lovely wife and friend Esther, who taught me to understand the importance of teamwork, particularly in the times when we faced the unknown side by side. There is no question in my heart that, despite my storied rise through the ranks, she is the true success of the two of us and has come to epitomize everything I see in a wife, mother, and friend. Her sacrifices, love, and street smarts led my children and me down the path of success. She is a model military wife, and my kids and I are who we are today because of her. She is a saint.

To my daughter Lori, who has followed in her mother's footsteps to become the very best at everything she does. She is a super mother, a loving daughter, and a great wife. She and Esther are true role models for what a great woman should be.

To my first grandchild Madison McCleskey, who finally taught me what true love is all about. Madison is treating me to all of the wonderful things I missed in my years of separation from my wife and daughter. I now understand the importance of these great women through my love affair with my granddaughter.

To all of the young officers and enlisted soldiers who continue to lead the way to our institution's great future. All of them taught me that if I looked after them, they would take care of me tenfold. Their devotion to Esther and me was unbelievable, unsurpassed, and the best thing that could have ever happened to us. They were all awesome soldiers, but they proved to be even greater friends. Esther and I owe these outstanding men and women everything. Hopefully, the guidance we offered, the passion we shared for soldiering and caring for military families, and our excitement for their future prospects was felt by them then and now.

I will dedicate all of the proceeds of this book to my educational foundation and to the soldiers and families who serve this great nation. A primer of our lives, this book was written for the sole purpose of helping the army realize its great future. While the book is critical of both the U.S. Army and American soldiers of Hispanic heritage, this narrative emerged out of the simple need to "tell it like it is." Much work needs to be done, and if this is the beginning of great changes, so be it. I enjoyed the great privilege of serving this nation and, if given the opportunity, I would do it all over again. I have been blessed to live the American dream, to be an American soldier, a humble veteran, and a better community leader. I hope that my small portion of our military history will enable others to enjoy the same blessings and opportunities I enjoyed.

On a personal note, I wish to thank the entire staff at BookPros for their time and effort toward this project and for their understanding of what it truly means for a soldier to write his story. Their collective efforts in editing, publishing, designing, printing, and publicizing brought this book to fruition. Without them I would have nothing. While I was giving dozens of speeches on Memorial Day and Veterans Day of 2007, visiting military hospitals around the world, and awarding scholarships from my educational foundation, the hard work of the staff at BookPros reminded me that Americans truly care.

This book is a collaborative work and tells the soldier's story to illustrate that freedom is not cheap, free, or negotiable. I just could not be grateful enough for our fighting men and women. Let it be known to the reader that these military studs and studettes have done right by our code of Duty, Honor, and Country. Their call to duty, their answer to the challenge, and their honorable service to their country deserve nothing less than a pause to reflect their devotion to duty. I personally salute and applaud their efforts, and I hope you do too, for Hispanic or not, we all bleed red.

Though there are 300 million Americans, less than 1 percent serve in uniform, and less than 7 percent claim veteran status. Thus the gift of freedom is magical for most and serious business for us few. And I simply ask that you keep our servicemen and women in your prayers.

The ultimate questions are, Do we Americans appreciate their sacrifices, and do we have the resolve to be patient enough to give them the time and support to execute the mission at hand? We owe them at least that. No one said it better than President Abraham Lincoln at his Second Inaugural in

March of 1865 when he said, "With malice toward none, with charity for all…let us strive on to finish the work we are in, to bind up the nation's wounds, to care for him who shall have borne the battle, and for his widow, and his orphan…"

General Valenzuela

I must first thank my esteemed co-author, Major General Alfred A. Valenzuela, for his friendship and encouragement as I worked with him on this endeavor. Early on in this project, I openly questioned myself as his choice to chronicle the legacy of Hispanic soldiers in the U.S. Army; after all, I was an Anglo-American who never served one day in uniform. With unwavering confidence, General Valenzuela explained that I had joined him in large part to provide the outsider's perspective that he felt this story needed. From the first day we began working together, it was clear that General Valenzuela didn't want this to be a fringe book, appealing only to military or Latino readers. He and I passionately believe that all Americans should understand the significance and unmistakable impact that Hispanic soldiers have made—and continue to make—on the direction of our country.

General V and his incredible family welcomed me into their lives with warmth and friendship. Every man or woman who climbs to a significant level of authority in the military possesses a discipline, an innate toughness that makes them a formidable ally and adversary. I now understand, however, that the truly great leaders also possess a human touch that inspires the soldiers who work and fight under their authority. General Valenzuela is clearly one of these great leaders. His guidance and friendship in our collaboration has been remarkable and inspiring, and I am eternally privileged as a writer to have been entrusted to tell this important story.

I must also thank Professor Jeffrey Addicott, the director of the Center for Terrorism Law at St. Mary's University School of Law for his leadership and assistance. Simply put, I never would have enjoyed the opportunity to work on this book without his professional mentorship. I would also like to thank the many teachers and professors who had enough confidence in my potential to challenge and inspire me to reach for the furthest stars. These are the teachers that truly made a difference in my life, and their efforts will never be forgotten.

I also thank my family and friends for their unwavering support and willingness to help me correct myself, when necessary. I am truly privileged to have grown up in a household and a community where the word "can't" has never been an acceptable currency in accounting for my personal shortcomings. My parents and siblings have always been my most vocal cheerleaders, and I will never discount the importance of their support.

Finally, I must thank my wife Laura for her unconditional love and confidence. Her patience and steadfast belief in me has buoyed me in my darkest moments. Because of this, she is the inspiration for everything I do. I am forever grateful for her love and friendship—it has saved my life.

Like General Valenzuela, I also dedicate this book to the men and women of the U.S. armed forces who continue to protect us with courage, dignity, and compassion. I believe that the United States boasts the greatest fighting force in the history of this planet, thanks in large part to the diversity of its soldiers. Simply put, the more inclusive these institutions are, the better equipped they will be to handle the challenges that arise in modern warfare. While Hispanic soldiers in the U.S. Army continue to face a number of challenges, I am confident that their future is bright.

Jason Lemons, J.D.

Of those who were instrumental in my army journey as a military wife, there is one person who stands above all—my sister Irene. She has been my confidant and shoulder to cry on, in addition to being a superb friend. She came to duty stations when I needed her, never failed to listen endlessly when I wanted to talk, and filled the void that my mother left when she passed. I am grateful for her help, indebted to her for her never-ending support, and honored to call her my sister.

Esther Valenzuela

INTRODUCTION

A Love Affair with Soldiering

In the 232-year history of the U.S. Army, Hispanic soldiers, beginning with Gen. Bernardo de Galvez of the U. S. Revolutionary War, have continually distinguished themselves by their selflessness and passion for their service. I have seen soldiers from every part of the spectrum come into our great army and blossom as competent soldiers, trusted friends, and most importantly, as men and women of the utmost courage, compassion, and integrity.

Each person joins the military for his or her own personal reason. Some join out of sheer patriotism or to carry on the warrior legacy that their family established generations ago. For others, the military represents a treasure trove of opportunities. They join in order to travel, obtain a better education, establish a career, or even set themselves out on the path to citizenship in this great nation. Many others join for reasons beyond altruism; in fact, some future heroes entered the military only after being presented with a jail-or-the-army choice from courts adopting an innovative approach to combating juvenile delinquency.

However, once someone enters the military, an amazing transformative experience occurs in which each person's own motivation for joining converts itself into an insatiable desire to serve. It's an amazing phenomenon to witness. These young men and women join our organization—often with reservations—and they blossom into great leaders. The military's personal impact creates a miraculous symbiotic relationship between the military and the individual. In other words, the military inspires each person to greater heights, and in turn, he or she propels the goals and the mission of the military to levels that were previously thought unattainable. Each member benefits from the training, skills, and personal focus that the military offers, but I dare say that the military incurs a much greater benefit in the work product of that person and, more importantly, the image of professionalism, compassion, and integrity that the individual conveys to others.

It doesn't matter what background people come from or what motivated them to join the military. They may have come in with the zeal of Nathan Hale, but it's just as likely that they joined through conscription, volunteering as their patriotic duty. More often than not, they come into the military and later find themselves embroiled in a lifelong love affair with military service. In my opinion, this passion develops because the U.S. military is often the only organization that sees the promise in these young men and women. Once the military cultivates the character of these brave people, they realize the true value of their decision to join, and their passion for service endures for the rest of their lives.

In addition, I think the passion to serve results from the optimism and tenaciousness that the military breeds in all its proud members. In a world that too often embraces cynicism and ironic detachment, the military celebrates and rewards the values that have made this nation great. More precisely, the military sees the potential in these young men and women, but it doesn't stop there. Instead, it nurtures their work ethic to the point that each person quickly develops a can-do attitude and a devotion to accomplishing the personal and institutional goals that are set out. As Theodore Roosevelt noted, "Criticism is necessary and useful; it is often indispensable; but it can never take the place of action, or even be a poor substitute for it. The function of the mere critic is of very subordinate usefulness. It is the doer of deeds who actually counts in the battle of life, and not the man who looks on and says how the fight ought to be fought, without himself sharing the stress and the danger." Our society too often encourages passivity and disconnection from the outside world; in my opinion, the military takes a different approach, rewarding the bold risk takers for the differences they make. This breeds even more enthusiasm for the mission and further cements the love affair each person shares with the military.

In the end, the professional military man or woman develops and endures because of mutual respect. The military respects the potential that each of its members possesses and is willing to provide the tools and training to turn that initial promise into results. In return, the individual respects the military for the significant investment—both financial and non-financial—that it made in his or her development as a warrior and as a person. And again, the symbiotic relationship between the military and the individual emerges. As long as each side of this equation appreciates the value of the other, this symbiosis will pay continual dividends that benefit our country everyday.

It should be noted that nobody signs up to die for his or her country. The death of a soldier is commonly attributed to accident, fate, destiny, or a number of other reasons that exist more for the purpose of comforting the living than to vindicate the dead. Regardless, these unsung heroes often find themselves at the intersection of happenstance and hell, and at that point the call for sacrifice is answered simply because that is the price that must be paid. In my thirty-three years of military experience, I have seen few, if any, who possess what could be characterized as a death wish; however, it is not uncommon for families to receive letters, e-mails, and phone calls from their sons or daughters that foreshadow their death. I can't explain exactly what it is that inspires these soldiers to prepare their families for their loss. It may be a premonition, but it's possible that they felt a duty to prepare their loved ones and reassure them that they accepted their fate, and they remained loyal to the mission. Regardless, their families will tell you—as they told me—that these individuals felt there was no choice but to confront their fate and lay down their lives in defense of their nation and their brothers and sisters in arms. These families are also reminders of the high cost of freedom—a price we are periodically required to pay in blood, suffering, and courage.

But what makes the Hispanic military man or woman special? What is it about them that stands out in relation to other members of our military? Why do the exploits of Hispanic soldiers remain largely unsung despite the fact that they stand among the most wounded and killed of any ethnic classification in the U.S. Army? And why, if their contributions to our military history are so easily quantifiable and their population within the U.S. is growing by leaps and bounds, do Hispanic soldiers lag so far behind when it comes to advancing to the flag officer and senior noncommissioned officer ranks?

This book will explore all of these questions later. But for now, I'll give you the general observation of Hispanic soldiers that I've developed in my career in the U.S. Army. In my experiences, Hispanic soldiers are special, because the selflessness and passion that they exhibit are more intense. Throughout the history of our nation, Hispanics have often been confronted with questions regarding their loyalty to this country and their willingness to contribute to American progress. Most of the time these questions are unfair and often borne of ignorance. But they become even more unreasonable when presented to the Hispanic soldier who has demonstrated his or her undying love for this nation and the opportunities it affords its citizens. When you consider that some Hispanic soldiers are not even U.S. citizens, it becomes more evident that these particular soldiers are the standard-bearers for the promise of America. They don't ask for handouts or special treatment; in fact, they're ready to pull up their sleeves and give everything they've got to accomplish the mission.

Hispanic soldiers also find themselves at a disadvantage because of the attributes that make them so valuable to the army. Hispanic soldiers, by and large, do not join for self-aggrandizement or personal gain. Sure, many of them enter the army to pursue a career that pays more than many of the options available to them back home. But it's increasingly rare to find Hispanic soldiers who aspire to move their way up the ranks to the higher echelons of army leadership; most of these soldiers just want to be among their comrades, helping to get the job done. In addition, many soldiers do not pursue the educational opportunities that become available to those who serve their country, even when these opportunities arise while they are still on active duty. Again, these soldiers would rather remain on the frontline, serving alongside the other men and women in their unit. We learned to be workhorses, not show horses.

The success of Hispanics in the army, therefore, should not be measured by their elevation to the general ranks; instead, one must look to the noncommissioned officer (NCO) corps to see the breadth of accomplishment of Hispanics in the army. Our lineage has been built by the Hispanic soldiers and NCOs who have stood on the frontlines and fought bravely for this nation for 232 years. In fact, I believe that Hispanic-American soldiers adhere to the concepts of honor and duty with an intensity that rivals that of any other soldier in the U.S. Army. But the question remains: are Hispanic soldiers victims of the attributes that make them so vital to the continuing success of the military?

Regardless of the questions we'll be exploring, it is indisputable that Hispanic soldiers are valuable and that their contributions are very important to the goals and missions of our military and nation. Their worth is proven in the example set by Sergeant José Mendoza Lopez, who fought in the Battle of the Bulge in World War II, and by other Medal of Honor recipients from Texas, California, and several other states, including Lucian Adams, Roy Benavidez, Cleto Rodriguez, Joe Rodriguez, and Louis Rocco.

This book was written to exalt the achievements and attributes of Hispanic soldiers in order to properly measure their value to the U.S. Army and our nation. That said, this book is not all sweetness and light; there are myriad challenges facing Hispanic Americans in the army or those considering a career in the armed forces. It is imperative that we demonstrate the value of education, self-discipline, integrity, and self-respect to the next generation—even if they have no interest in pursuing a career in the military. Just as Hispanic soldiers have played an invaluable role in the successes of our military, Hispanic Americans continue to make awesome contributions to the greatness of our nation. I want to honor their gifts and see their incredible legacy continue for generations onward.

I begin my study of the legacy of Hispanic soldiers by reflecting on the bravery and loyalty of noncitizen soldiers. After that, I will spend some time highlighting some of the more notable moments in my career—in part, to reassure today's soldiers that I understand the challenges they face everyday. In addition, my wife and children have generously penned separate chapters that provide guidance and support to the families of soldiers.

I will then discuss the importance of improving the diversity of the army and the challenges that must be faced in making this improvement.

In the final chapter, I return to the impressive legacy of our Hispanic soldiers. I discuss the many challenges that these soldiers face and the challenges that the military must overcome in order to remain relevant to our soldiers. I won't flinch in my criticism of our soldiers or the army, but I pledge that all of my observations will be made fairly and with an emphasis on the long-term health of our great military and our extraordinary nation.

CHAPTER 1

THE ALPHA AND THE OMEGA: HONORING THE UNSUNG
SOLDIERS

Wars may be fought with weapons, but they are won by men.
                              —Gen. George S. Patton

Burying Specialist Rodrigo Gonzalez-Garza

For a fleeting moment as I stood on the edge of the Texas–Mexico border, doubts began to creep in, and I wondered whether I was in over my head. The ethereal early morning moonlight illuminated the still-slumbering city of Nuevo Laredo, Mexico, and this quiet moment gave me a chance to meditate on the events that brought me here, standing next to the casket of Specialist Rodrigo Gonzalez-Garza, the first soldier killed in the Iraq War.

Because I was one of only a handful of generals in the army who spoke Spanish, the Pentagon chose me to preside over Specialist Gonzalez's funeral, and I was well aware of the gravity and importance of the assignment. Moreover, I was aware that a number of diverse parties were interested in how well I performed in this endeavor. However, the criteria they used to evaluate my performance varied just as much as the groups themselves. For one, Gonzalez's family wanted and deserved a dignified proceeding that befitted the hero their son had become. Second, the U.S. Army relied on me to be its ambassador at the funeral—to show the mourners that Specialist Gonzalez's sacrifice served a higher purpose and that the country for which he fought was grateful for his service. But other interested parties had converged on this proceeding, ensuring that this funeral—for one of the first casualties of the Iraq War—would be challenging and unforgettable.

Specialist Rodrigo Gonzalez-Garza, known as "Gonzo" to his fellow soldiers, died in a training accident in Kuwait on February 25, 2003. Born in Sabinas Hidalgo, a moderately sized city in Nuevo Leon, Mexico, Rodrigo moved with his family to San Antonio when he was young. He graduated from Fox Tech Vocational High School in San Antonio in 1996 and joined the army the following year. The army, as it often does with so many young men and women, allowed Rodrigo to discover his potential as a man. Full of life, his quick wit and restless energy won him many friends among his peers. His leadership, selflessness, and courage also won him many admirers in the army. Furthermore, his dynamic personality belied a gentle and nurturing spirit. For example, one of his best friends in the army recalled the way Rodrigo embraced his family when he would visit them. Rodrigo slept in the spare bedroom, which was the baby's room, and if the baby would cry during the night, he would get up and take care of him.

Gonzalez was a UH-60 Black Hawk crew chief with Company A of the Fifth Battalion, 158th Aviation Regiment, assigned to Fifth Corp out of Germany and staged in Kuwait. When he joined the army in 1997, he started out as an airborne infantryman and was later reclassified. A hardworking and committed member of his unit, he loved flying with his pilot, Chief Warrant Officer 2 Tim Moehling. On the night of February 24, 2003, Gonzalez's crew received a "be prepared" order that, at the time, indicated the growing likelihood of a potential invasion of Iraq. The crew, which included Gonzalez, Moehling, and two members of another unit, were engaged in night combat maneuvers to rehearse their upcoming key role of aviation support and operations. When someone attempted to switch Gonzalez to a different flight, he insisted on remaining with his pilot and his crew. Shortly after midnight, an unexpected sandstorm overwhelmed their helicopter as it flew low over the desert floor. All four men were killed when the helicopter smashed into the ground seconds later.

Rodrigo's death carried significance on multiple levels. First, these fallen soldiers would be remembered as the first casualties of the Iraq War. For better or worse, Specialist Rodrigo Gonzalez-Garza's name would be placed at the very front of the list of Iraq casualties. On another level, Gonzalez's death came at a time when the army was ushering in changes in the way it conducted the funerals of its fallen soldiers. Most notably, the Pentagon—at the urging of the U.S. Army—decreed that a flag officer (army general) would be required to attend and preside over each funeral for soldiers killed in Iraq. The White House and the military establishment looked at this as an opportunity to properly honor these heroes and avoid the mistakes that may have diminished the service of soldiers during the Vietnam era. It was imperative that each presiding general honor the sacrifices of the deceased with dignity and decorum. Moreover, the presiding general was expected to act as an agent for the army and the American people in expressing gratitude and sympathy to the families of these soldiers. Still, there were other important aspects surrounding Rodrigo's life and death that would not become evident until later.

Because of the gravity of the proceedings, preparations for a military funeral are never easy. But thanks to explicit directions from the U.S. Department of Defense, the service itself is not difficult to set up. Every military funeral must follow the same general format, consisting at a minimum of the sounding of "Taps" and the ceremonial folding and presentation of the American flag to the fallen soldier's next of kin. In addition, any eulogy given by a service representative at the ceremony must pay proper respects and demonstrate the gratitude of the nation for the soldier's service and sacrifice. The Department of Defense sums up the purpose of the formal military funeral thusly: "rendering military funeral honors reflects the high regard and respect accorded to military service and demonstrates military professionalism to the nation and the world."[1]

The real challenge in preparing for a military funeral comes in understanding and properly responding to the needs of the soldier's family at that time. The Department of Defense requires those presiding over the funeral to "respond expeditiously and sensitively to requests for military funeral support."[2] This matter-of-fact language disguises the fact that the wishes of the family in their time of grief are often difficult to carry out. However, these challenges do not overshadow the great honor and privilege of taking part in the military honors of Specialist Rodrigo Gonzalez. I personally owe Secretary of the Army Louis Caldera and General Eric Shinseki a debt of gratitude in assigning me the honor of representing the U.S. Army in the funeral of a great military hero. This privilege would affect my life personally and further strengthen the pride I have in the U.S. Army as an institution that cares for and honors all of its heroes. I presided over twenty other funerals over the following year, and each of them, though different and special in their own individual way, replicated the honor I felt when I participated in that first ceremony.

When I first contacted Rodrigo's parents, Ramiro and Orelia Gonzalez, I could sense their sadness and feelings of loss. But it was clear that both of them were very proud of the man their son had become and of what he did to serve his adopted country, even though he was not yet a U.S. citizen. When I asked them what I could do to honor the memory of Rodrigo, they replied with three requests. First, they informed me that they had three other sons in the army and wanted to bring them home for the funeral. Second, they requested that San Antonio's beloved Archbishop Patrick Flores perform the viewing and rosary ceremony. Finally, they asked that their son be buried in the country in which he was born—Mexico.

Immediately, I feared that their first request could not be fulfilled, due to the logistical wrangling that would be needed to get three soldiers in three separate locations back for a funeral. Additionally, the fact that the army was in the process of ramping up its preparations for the war in Iraq that would begin later in March made this wish difficult to fulfill. When I contacted my superiors, I was pleasantly surprised by their immediate willingness to bring these men home for their fallen brother's funeral and their subsequent decision to reassign each of them in order to keep them closer to their family. I was also pleased to learn that Archbishop Flores would be available to perform the service.

What an honor it was to meet the entire Gonzalez family a few days later at the funeral home in San Antonio. They introduced me to Rodrigo's three brothers: Staff Sergeant Ramiro Gonzalez, an army recruiter in Laredo; Rodrigo's twin brother Sergeant Ricardo Gonzalez, a combat medic stationed in Fort Drum, New York, who was subsequently assigned to Iraq; and Private First Class Rolando Gonzalez, the youngest brother and an operating room technician stationed at West Point, New York. I was also introduced to Rodrigo's older sister, Veronica Valadez. After meeting these outstanding individuals, I marveled at the strong American values that had been instilled in each of these children, even though none of them were American citizens at the time. They still had great pride in their Mexican heritage, but they believed that good citizenship and national contribution knew no borders. In their time of grief, this extraordinary family embraced me and assured me that they understood the importance and value of Rodrigo's sacrifice. They all knew that he died honorably and for a good cause. It has been said that the army recruits soldiers and retains families. With that in mind, I left their home even more determined to do the right thing for the most patriotic family I had encountered during my military career so far.

The church service and military honors ceremony held at Fort Sam Houston National Cemetery the next day honored Rodrigo in a way that brought great solace to the Gonzalez family and their friends in San Antonio, Texas. Representatives from every branch of the U.S. armed services showed up to pay their respects, and the large turnout of servicemen and women overwhelmed the family. The impressive turnout that day went beyond just the call of duty—most of these men and women considered Rodrigo to be a cherished friend, and they wanted to honor him both as a soldier and as a person. A curious media attended these services and found a stoic family mourning the loss of their son while maintaining pride in his service and sacrifice.

My eulogy touched on common themes that I revisited in later services. I first discussed the military funeral honors and the significance of these traditions as rites that not only honor our fallen heroes but also inspire the rest of us to live up to their sacrifice. I also reminded the attendees that, although it is hard to stomach the loss of a great man and hero like Rodrigo Gonzalez, he died serving our nation in the most important way possible—protecting our freedom.

On a personal level, my experiences in honoring, eulogizing, and praying for these soldiers and their families in English and Spanish gave me a new perspective on the significance of my cultural upbringing. I proudly and confidently explicated in two languages what it meant for these soldiers to serve in the U.S. Army. I felt it important to pay tribute to Rodrigo in both English and Spanish to ensure that no part of his story was lost in translation, so to speak.

The family's final request—to bury their son in his hometown of Sabinas Hidalgo, Mexico—was the most difficult to carry out. After all, the United States and Mexico had been engaged in a very public disagreement regarding the necessity for military action in Iraq. Relations between the two countries chilled precipitously after Mexico voted against the U.N. resolution authorizing the use of force in Iraq. Public opinion in Mexico was strongly against the war, due in part to a culture that often assesses the fervor of one's Mexican nationalism by the zeal of their opposition to the policies of the United States. Because of these tensions, I worried that the Gonzalez family's decision to bury their son in Mexico carried the risk of allowing an ugly brand of politics to enter what needed to be a somber, respectful ceremony.

A call to the United States Embassy in Mexico highlighted more international concerns. They informed me that under no circumstances was I to allow the body of Specialist Gonzalez to cross the border visibly wearing the uniform of a U.S. Army soldier or with the American flag draped over the casket. In addition, Rodrigo's brothers and I were encouraged not to wear our military uniforms, and I was discouraged from presenting the U.S. flag to the family at the burial service. A careless error on my part during the funeral, regardless of intent, could be taken as a serious affront to the dignity of Mexico. I was eventually given permission to wear my dress green class A uniform after negotiations with the U.S. Embassy in Mexico and Northern Command, the newly established command center in Colorado Springs responsible for security of the United States, the Canadian and Mexican borders, and parts of the Caribbean and contiguous sections of the Atlantic and Pacific Oceans. But the more we discussed these matters, the more I feared that we were planning a funeral in the middle of a hornet's nest of longstanding political tensions between two proud nations.

On the day of the funeral, as I crossed the border into Mexico, I looked out on Nuevo Laredo and the area surrounding it and realized that I would have to rise to all of the challenges that stood before me. I owed it to Rodrigo, his incredible family, the army, and myself to ensure that everyone who attended his second round of military honors and burial understood the importance of this soldier's service and sacrifice. The willingness of young men and women who were born in Mexico to fight for their adopted country had long puzzled many Mexicans. It was my duty to demonstrate, through Rodrigo's example, what it means to be an American—and a Hispanic-American.

The army motto on the battlefield implores us to leave no soldier behind, and I wasn't about to leave Rodrigo or his legacy behind, no matter what. I was determined to stand my ground, wear my uniform, and proudly honor his sacrifice. Any later repercussions would have to take a backseat to the proper honors and burial of this American—and Mexican—hero.

Nestled halfway between Nuevo Laredo and Monterrey, Sabinas Hidalgo is a small mining community populated by roughly twenty-five thousand people. It is buttressed by the Sierra De La Iguana and Sierra De Gomes mountain ranges in the west and abuts the Sabinas River. On our journey south, I was filled with concern that the community would not be hospitable to one of its sons who embraced American life in so many ways. My worries were surprisingly unnecessary.

As we approached Sabinas Hidalgo that morning, we soon found ourselves on a road flanked by people on both sides enthusiastically waving American and Mexican flags. They were mourning the loss of one of their sons, but their mood also seemed to include feelings of national *orgullo* (pride) and reverent *agradecimiento* (gratitude). Putting politics and any cultural issues aside, they had converged on this road to celebrate the life of a true hero. The funeral was no different; everyone there respected the gravity of the occasion and Rodrigo's sacrifice. The standing-room-only crowds at the church and the cemetery knew he was a hero, regardless of the flag he fought for and the country he considered his home. The residents of Sabinas Hidalgo also maintained their own municipal pride, knowing that they played a significant part in molding this fine man. As I watched this community come out to honor its fallen son, I thought of the well-known African proverb, "It takes a village to raise a child." The people of Sabinas Hidalgo exemplified the meaning of this maxim and had reason to be proud of the hero they helped raise.

As we made our way to the cemetery, I became acquainted with the Mexican custom of stopping at significant sites in the life of the deceased, such as the birthplace and any other locations that the deceased called home. As we stopped at Rodrigo's birth home, I gained an even deeper appreciation for this custom and my own Hispanic heritage. This tradition reflects a deep understanding among the Mexican people that the sum of a person's life is not always easily quantifiable and is often better understood by considering and honoring all significant things in the life of the deceased. After viewing Rodrigo's childhood home, I knew this exceptional man even better.

When we reached the dirt road to the cemetery, the family walked in procession all the way to the gravesite. From a distance, we could see two flagpoles surrounded by scores of people. On one flagpole, the Mexican flag waved at half-mast. The other flagpole was bare. After we got out of our cars, the eldest brother, Staff Sergeant Ramiro Gonzalez, informed me that they had brought the American flag and were prepared to hoist it up the other flagpole to honor Rodrigo. Ramiro looked me in the eye and reminded me that we had come too far to censor our pride in Rodrigo. "Sir, don't back down now," implored Ramiro, "you honored us with your presence—now help us honor Rodrigo."

But by that point, I wasn't sure whether Ramiro was summoning my inner strength or if it was actually an angel—or even Rodrigo—inspiring me to stand my ground. Whoever it was, I stood taller in my uniform at that moment and was determined to pay tribute to Rodrigo the way we honor all of our fallen brothers—with unapologetic pride. Nothing was going to stop me from showing every person in attendance how the U.S. Army honors its soldiers.

After the casket was removed from the hearse, the three brothers—all proudly wearing their class A uniforms—unfolded and raised the American flag up the flagpole, resting it at half-mast. This act triggered a round of applause and cheers from the crowd. As both flags flew proudly in the breeze, I marveled at the convergence of these diverse groups of people who all felt the need to pay their respects to Rodrigo. There was no animosity, no bitterness; instead, we found ourselves in a community of people who were proud that four of their sons had so ably and honorably served in the U.S. Army.

After the funeral, I was honored to meet a number of local Mexican veterans who had also proudly served in the U.S. Army in World War II, Korea, and Vietnam. They too were heartened by our decision to honor Rodrigo's service in Sabinas Hidalgo with full military honors. They were very appreciative of my presence; in fact, these gentlemen protectively flanked me after the funeral as I answered questions from the local media. The local press was transfixed on trivial issues that bypassed the more important lessons of that day. Their questions revolved around pecuniary details, including how much money the family was entitled to from the United States government. The veterans surrounding me grew impatient with this line of questioning, occasionally interjecting scolding reminders that this day was devoted to the duty of laying a fallen brother to rest. To these men, I remained their brother—regardless of our differences in culture, class, and nationality.

These men reminded me that the bond between soldiers is sacrosanct, and it transcends almost everything, including politics. We were truly a band of brothers, and Rodrigo's passing reminded all of us of the unyielding strength of the soldier's bond.

In the end, this was a diplomatic victory for the United States and an important personal reminder that we should never shy away from honoring the people who make up the U.S. Army. This institution has a proud history of standing up for justice and freedom; to shrink away from who we are and what we have accomplished tarnishes the memories of the men and women before us who have served this institution. If the U.S. Army had tried to minimize its presence at the proceedings that day, it would have sent a dangerous message that we didn't really believe in our mission and the sacrifices of our soldiers. It would have been easy to succumb to fear on that day, but I knew in my heart that the only way to pay proper tribute to Rodrigo was by giving him and his family full military honors. After all, politics should never trump our instincts to do the right thing.

Not long after the funeral, I learned that Rodrigo had applied for U.S. citizenship shortly before his death. It was amazing to think that a man who had served the United States so selflessly was not even a citizen of the country he defended. Apparently, other government officials felt the same way, because Rodrigo was posthumously granted citizenship status. Moreover, all of Rodrigo's brothers eventually became American citizens, too.

Exactly one year after his death, his sister gave birth to a son—a native-born citizen of the country he gave his life for. She named him Rodrigo, further ensuring that Specialist Gonzalez's legacy would carry on into the next generation of Hispanic Americans. To me, this event completed his story in the cycle of life; the alpha, or beginning, of young Rodrigo's life, marked the omega, or end, of his uncle's life.

Noncitizen Soldiers

After learning of Rodrigo's noncitizen status, I decided to do some research and discovered that of the forty-two Hispanic Medal of Honor recipients, four were not American citizens at the time of their heroic actions. These brave individuals, despite their noncitizen status, were still recognized for bravery beyond the call of duty in the name of their adopted home.

Despite this, Hispanic soldiers are often portrayed as persons wrangling with competing loyalties. As one mother-in-law of a noncitizen soldier put it, "Mexicans in the U.S. Army are trapped between two walls—they have Mexican heritage on one hand and duty to the United States on the other. It's a very hard place to be." It is common for Hispanic soldiers in general, and Mexicans specifically, to feel as if they are pulled in a number of directions. They fight simultaneous but conflicting notions that they are not "Hispanic enough" for the people they grew up with and not "American enough" for the people they work with.

Life in the army is difficult for noncitizens, who often find themselves not only proving their loyalty to the country they have chosen to fight for, but also fighting immigration policies that fail to take their service into proper account. How ironic it is that these people, who courageously answer the call to serve this nation and who literally yearn to be Americans, find themselves and their loved ones forced to live on the fringes of our society. But despite the obstacles that noncitizen soldiers face, I have always found them to be brave and loyal fighters who just want to prove themselves on the front. I believe that the U.S. Army is a stronger institution, thanks to their service and contribution.

Remembering the Lives of Our Fallen Heroes

In 1962, President John F. Kennedy spoke to graduating cadets of the U.S. Military Academy, in which he warned of a burgeoning breed of warfare that threatened freedom lovers everywhere:

> This is another type of war, new in its intensity, ancient in its origin—war by guerillas, subversives, insurgents, assassins, war by ambush instead of by combat; by infiltration, instead of aggression, seeking victory by eroding and exhausting the enemy instead of engaging him…It requires in those situations where we must counter it, and these are the kinds of challenges that will be before us in the next decade if freedom is to be saved, a whole new kind of strategy, a wholly different kind of force, and therefore a new and wholly different kind of military training.

None of the soldiers I buried were innately prepared for the cruel nature of warfare that they were up against; however, they trained tirelessly and were ultimately prepared to protect our nation against any and all enemies.

The Hispanic soldiers whom I had the honor of burying and memorializing were all beautiful, exceptional souls. None of them took themselves too seriously, but they took their roles in life very seriously. To all of them, failing to fulfill their commitment would be a personal affront, and the fear of failing motivated and resonated within each of them. In the end, their sacrifice is translated into freedom; indeed, it is their incalculable gift to the rest of us. The respect and honor they have brought to the Hispanic community is but another part of the unpayable debt that they bestowed on the rest of us.

Unfortunately, the fact that we know so little about these heroes is the continuing tragedy that accompanies their legacy; that being said, I hope these words will reverse that drought. After all, Hispanics and Americans alike should be proud of the legacy of these soldiers.

The feelings I experienced when I buried American soldiers killed in war were intense and overwhelming. The grief of the families and friends of the fallen hero is stark and real, and I could not help but feel the intense sorrow that pervaded the proceedings. But as I considered the heroism of these soldiers, the indescribable plethora of emotions unified my spirit as a member of the U.S. Army, and I was left to simply stand in awe of the heroism and sacrifices of these men and women.

The following soldiers who gave their lives were common folks who found themselves in nearly unfathomable situations. I am always astonished when I consider what these young men and women did when it truly counted. Suffice it to say, the character of these heroes was forged in the fog of war, the heat of battle, and the whir of bullets, but they never let this nation down. We all owe it to them to reflect on what their lives might have been, but never will be. We simply cannot allow ourselves as a society to take for granted the bravery of these soldiers, for their acts of heroism give true meaning to the very freedoms that define us. If we allow their courage to go unappreciated, then we truly have committed a regrettable act of sacrilege, and we are undeserving of their demonstration of no greater love. What they gave us is our personal mandate; America's challenge is to remember. These are my inspirations:

Pfc. Steven Acosta was a bright young man who grew up in the fruit fields of California. A hard worker, Steven was always available to help his father labor in the fields to help feed their family. He answered the army's call out of an innate need to serve his country, but he also looked forward to returning home to enroll in college. At his memorable funeral, Steven's low-rider friends came out en masse to bid him farewell. Although his buddies appeared a little rough around the edges, I could see the true depth of their character by the reverent tones they used when they spoke of their fallen brother. They came to ensure that Steven was sent off in the right way and was never forgotten. It seemed like the entire city of Calexico turned out for his funeral and reception. Although a common sight at Hispanic funerals, a mariachi band celebrated Steven's short, but memorable, life with a number of traditional Mexican folk songs. To be sure, his loss was difficult for the family. But his spirit of kindness and leadership was beautifully evidenced by his decision to have his insurance money go to his sister to pay for her education.

An accomplished high school athlete, **Sgt. Michael Paul Barrera** exuded confidence and charisma. He, like so many others, joined the Army to defend his country, and he did just that in Kosovo and Iraq. He had a detailed plan for his life, but he selflessly put his personal ambitions behind his need to serve others. A valued member of an M1 tank crew, he had the utmost confidence in his state-of-the-art armored vehicle and their well-trained crew. The other members of his unit praised his leadership, street smarts, and vision. I have never seen an outpouring of friends and admirers like I did on the solemn day of his funeral in Von Ormy, Texas. Today, a school that was named in memory of him is the pride and joy of the community, ensuring that not a day goes by in which Sgt. Barrera's sacrifice is forgotten.

Spc. Richard Arriaga of Ganado, Texas was a standout student who decided after 9/11 that it was his duty to answer the call of his country. While he never met his newborn daughter Bianca Mia, it was clear that he had what it took to be an excellent father. One obituary recounted that when Spc. Arriaga would call home, he would tell his family members to pick up his daughter and show her the love and attention that he couldn't while he was halfway around the world. His funeral in Ganado was like so many I attended, one in which the entire town appeared to bid him farewell and express their gratitude for his sacrifice.

Another woman who rose fast in the ranks of the army, **Staff Sgt. Melissa Valles** lost her life while serving on a logistical mission. Her comrades remembered her as someone who always showed proper respect and decorum and pushed the troops in her unit to be their best. Although only slightly over five feet in stature, her dogged determination and leadership gave her all the credibility she needed. The city of Eagle Pass was devastated upon hearing the news of her passing. In fact, people came from across the Mexican border to pay their respects. Sadly, she left behind an eight-year-old son.

Pfc. Analaura Esparza-Gutierrez was raised outside of Houston, Texas. After she completed basic training, her proud family drove to Ft. Hood every weekend to visit their only daughter. She joined the army with the ambition that it would be her springboard to a college education. She was also engaged to a fellow soldier and hoped to get married after she returned from Iraq. Not normally a convoy driver, Analaura volunteered on that fateful day to replace a sick comrade. She was killed when her convoy was hit by a roadside bomb near the U.S. base established in Tikrit. White doves were released at her funeral, which flew heavenward, only to return to her casket. This display surprised the crowd, but Analaura deserved the peace and dignity that God and her parents gave her that solemn day. Although Analaura's parents were elderly and spoke very little English, they poignantly accepted her death with pride and composure, intimating to me that, although her life was painfully short, she emerged from this world a true hero.

The sudden, unexpected death of **Spc. Zeferino Eusebio Colunga** was difficult for the people who knew and loved him. Known by family and friends as "Cowboy," Zeferino made quite a name for himself at Bellville High School as a formidable tackle on the football team and as a quiet, intelligent leader who graduated with honors. After graduation, he sought a career in the army as a way to help support his family, who had emigrated from Mexico. This was a difficult decision, as his father had been recently deported, and his mother and sister, who was, incidentally, the only U.S. citizen in their family, were left to fend for themselves in Texas. Zeferino's last letter home recognized the family's struggle to live and thrive as an incomplete unit. Before he closed this letter, Cowboy told his family that if something were to happen to him, he wanted his insurance money to go to his sister to help her attend college and nursing school. Zeferino died on August 6, 2003 after a battle with pneumonia and acute leukemia that began shortly after he arrived in Kuwait. Recognizing the depth of Zeferino's contribution to his community, his hometown rallied in support of the family. Shortly afterwards, Bellville High School retired Zeferino's football jersey number. Sadly, his father was again deported after the funeral. The father's picture was taken at the funeral, which alerted the authorities to his reentry into the United States to bury his son.

Staff Sgt. Hector R. Perez was the elder statesman of the group of soldiers I buried. An infantryman at his core, he proudly served as one of the celebrated Screaming Eagles of the 101st Airborne Division. He chose to serve out of respect and admiration for his father's valiant service in World War II. Hector left behind a strong army wife and three gorgeous daughters, all of whom had a whimsical, yet close and meaningful relationship with their father. The only brother to a dedicated group of sisters, Hector was the mainstay of his family, or "el consentido de la familia," the favorite son. He is remembered by his comrades as a two-time war veteran who knew all the maneuvers and made it his goal to get all of his soldiers back safely. But the soldiers who knew Hector also remember his softer side. He loved handing out all the candy he received from family care packages to local children, and he sent home pictures that, more often than not, consisted of the handsome faces of children who lived in the villages and countryside he patrolled. While a few unfortunate and unintended misunderstandings beset his funeral, the army will continue to champion his leadership and his sacrifice.

Upon joining the army, **Spc. Jose Amancio Perez III** only asked his family to place his army portrait on the wall of his grandparents' home alongside that of his late uncle Billy Benavides, who served in the Gulf War. Eager to help others, Jose was a respected combat medic who became the inspiration of his family and his community. The good people of San Diego, Texas, came out en masse to pay their respects and honor a young man they remembered as a good student with a playful sense of humor. Jose was destined for greatness, and the whole city knew it. He truly made his mark in the army, earning the Bronze Star, a Purple Heart, and the Combat Medical Badge in his three-year career. Although his death during an ambush in Taji, Iraq, was tragic, Jose's comrades praised his bravery in responding to the attack and his attempt to save as many of his brothers as possible. He is the epitome of a son, student, and soldier, and his good nature and heroism will be remembered in the annals of the army forever.

Spc. Robert Arsiaga is remembered as someone who understood his place in the army. He told his friends and family that this was his job, and as long as he did things the right way, the Iraqi people had a fighting chance at a better life. Hailing from Midland, Texas, Robert actually studied drafting before he enlisted and dreamt of building a dream house for his mother. Once he joined the army, he gave it everything he had and distinguished himself as a good, valiant soldier. At the same time, he looked forward to returning home and starting a family with his young wife, Tracie. Their hopes were dashed on April 4, 2004, when his convoy was ambushed outside of Sadr City. Robert and Tracie had been married only five months.

Since they first met at Fort Hood, **Spc. Israel Garza** and Spc. Robert Arsiaga were inseparable, almost like brothers. It would have been easy for the casual observer to assume that Israel and Robert *were* brothers. They were the same age, they were both married, and they both grew up near each other in west Texas—Robert hailed from Midland, and Israel was from Lubbock. They even resembled each other, so much so that they would occasionally switch clothes to tease their comrades. As they lived like brothers, they also died like brothers. They fought alongside one another when Shiite militiamen attacked their convoy in Sadr City. Israel left behind his wife, three sons, and a daughter.

Beatriz Carballo spoke to her husband **Spc. Adolfo C. Carballo** on her cell phone just hours before he was killed in heavy combat in Baghdad. He had assured her that he was doing fine and looking forward to that night's dinner after he had completed a mission that day. Sadly, Beatriz learned later that Adolfo died from injuries he had sustained when shrapnel struck him in a firefight later that night. Adolfo had distinguished himself in the ROTC program at John H. Reagan High School in Houston, Texas. Although he felt that he fit in the military, he looked forward to the day that he could come home and join the Houston Police Department. In his conversations with his young wife, Adolfo told her that he liked his job in the army, but he was ready for the day when he could be with her and enjoy a carefree life again.

When he was five years old, **Pfc. Rey D. Cuervo** envisioned his future in the army and told his mother Rosalba all about his dream of becoming a soldier. Although she was surprised at his early ambition, Rosalba was never surprised later on that her driven son had fulfilled his promise. Rey lived for his family, never allowing the distance between them to keep them from communicating with each other. He sent money home so his parents could buy a computer to e-mail him more often. He also bought a camera so he could share his experiences with all of the people he left behind in Laguna Vista, Texas. Rey was a professional soldier, and he approached his job with great vigor and enthusiasm. But he missed life in Texas, even telling his mother that he could almost smell the Whataburgers that he had left behind. Rey was killed on December 28, 2003, when an improvised explosive device hit the vehicle he was riding in outside Baghdad. Rey's memorial service was a crowded affair; more than 100 friends and family members came to pay their respects to a man they remembered as unselfish and friendly. As sudden and tragic as his death was, Rey almost preternaturally understood that his number could be called at any moment. In fact, before he left for Iraq, he warned his mother that he probably would not return from the place where he was going.

Pfc. Pablo Manzano was the consummate soldier; his first team leader recalls Pablo possessing everything you hoped for in a new private, including intelligence, motivation, and a positive spirit that could keep the entire team's morale up. A 2002 graduate of Southwest High School in El Centro, California, he was also the revered only son of his family. He had a positive impact on everyone in his family, from parents to siblings on down to the six-year-old cousin who relished having Pablo as a wrestling partner during family get-togethers. His family had implored Pablo to request a transfer to a different, safer area, one where he would be kept away from more dangerous operations. Pablo reassured them, telling him that he was doing well, but also telling them that he wasn't willing to leave the other members of his company.

The men and women who served with **Sgt. Juan M. Serrano** of Manati, Puerto Rico, remember him as a faithful soldier and a trusted teacher to his troops. He lost his life on July 24, 2003, when he was changing a tire on an M998 vehicle in Baghdad. The truck fell on him as he was at work, inflicting a fatal head injury. Soldiers are regularly trained to use a safety cage when inflating tires to prevent injury if a rim were to pop off. There was initially some question whether Sgt. Serrano followed these protocols, but eyewitnesses later confirmed that he performed his duties properly in the course of correcting one of his soldier's initial errors. He lived his life selflessly, always seeking to bestow wisdom and know-how on his troops; ultimately, he gave his life in the same manner. He had everything we treasure in our awesome NCOs, and he will remain a model of a valiant soldier for future generations.

It seemed like **Sgt. Gerardo Moreno** of Terrell, Texas, had a million friends. Better known by friends and family as "Chito," Gerardo was praised for his big heart and the ease in which he could turn strangers into friends. He lost his life on April 6, 2004, when a rocket-propelled grenade was fired on his unit outside of Ashula, Iraq. Ever the soldier, he was on foot patrol when his unit came under siege. He joined the army in 1999 and left behind an impressive array of admiring friends both in and outside of the army.

At an early age, **Pfc. Armando Soriano** developed a reputation as a tireless worker and faithful son. He was always willing to do odd jobs in restaurants and construction areas around his hometown of Houston to help his parents make ends meet. His friends and family all remembered him as someone who thought of others before himself, and he initially joined the army to help his parents and to learn about the world around him. Despite his mother's initial objections, he joined the army almost immediately after he graduated from high school. Armando knew that a life in the army was his ticket to a better life for his family and himself, and he told his parents that the decision to enlist was his and his alone. His mother came around when she saw the man that emerged from basic training. She beamed with pride when she realized that he had become a man of substance and a force for positive change in the world. Armando was tragically killed on February 1, 2004, when inclement weather conditions in Haditha, Iraq, caused his vehicle to slip off the road and flip over. His family remembered him as unselfish and strong; his comrades and friends remembered him as the very best soldier they knew. Armando joined the army largely to help his family become U.S. citizens. How ironic it was that, after his death, his father Enrique Soriano's government-sanctioned green card was revoked due to a prior deportation. I am grateful to the efforts of Congressman Gene Green and others who continue to work to right this injustice and allow a father to continue to live in the country that his son gallantly gave his life for.

Cpl. Tomas Sotelo was, in the words of the commander of his training unit at Ft. Polk, a "guiding light." He was the type of soldier that every unit needs to be successful; in fact, the cohesiveness of the unit depends on people like Tomas, who put the group first and who ingratiate themselves with everyone in the unit. He always found ways to counsel the younger soldiers in need of guidance or a big brother figure. Tomas was also the kind of person who knew how to lighten the mood of one person or the entire group with a compliment or a joke. He was the proud owner of an individual DVD player, but he was happiest using it when a crowd gathered around that small screen to enjoy a movie. His friends back home in Houston knew the same gregarious man—a friend and trusted leader to all, and the subject of more than a few crushes at Reagan High School. He was lost on June 27, 2003, when a rocket-propelled grenade hit the vehicle in his convoy outside of Baghdad. Although the depth of his loss is inestimable, I have faith that another young soldier, inspired by his example, will become the same trusted leader, counselor, and friend that Tomas was.

Life in the army was a family affair for **Spc. Ramon Reyes-Torres**. Inspired by his grandfather's twenty-four-year career in the military, Ramon enlisted fresh out of high school. His grandfather, Carmelo Reyes, swelled with pride for his grandson's accomplishments in the coming years. Ramon distinguished himself as a humble and dedicated soldier who treated his career as if his family's honor depended on it. He was killed in Baghdad on July 16, 2003, as he attempted to shelter himself from a nearby vehicle containing a command-detonated device. He was buried next to his grandfather in his family's tomb in Caguas, Puerto Rico.

I also buried two Anglo soldiers who are as deserving of recognition and remembrance as any of the other soldiers I buried. Because of their faithful service to country and their bravery in the face of death, I proudly include them in my list of exemplary heroes who gave everything they had for the rest of us.

The people who knew **Chief Warrant Officer 2 (CW2) Lawrence S. (Shane) Colton** described him as an army lifer. A native of Oklahoma City, Shane had spent over twelve years in the army, and he couldn't imagine a better or more fulfilling life for himself. Because of this, he carried an infectious optimism that helped inspire his outfit to reach for greater heights. His optimism was captured in a news release that included some words from Shane. He assured people back home that "life's not so bad [in Iraq]," and that his team was "well-suited for the mission." Shane and his co-pilot CWO3 Wesley C. Fortenberry were killed when their Apache helicopter was hit by enemy rocket fire as they made a final pass toward the enemy in order to provide air support to the 706th Support Battalion, which came under attack while it was taking fuel to Marines in Fallujah. The army posthumously awarded both men with the Distinguished Flying Cross, which recognizes "heroism or extraordinary achievement while participating in an aerial flight." This heroic duo was recognized further on December 9, 2005, when Army Vice Chief of Staff Gen. Richard A. Cody helped dedicate the Fortenberry/Colton Physical Fitness Center at Fort Rucker, Alabama. Remembering their sacrifice, General Cody noted that "[t]heir unwavering steadiness saved other soldiers, and they were never deterred from their mission."

The story of **Spc. Tracy L. Laramore** reminds me of Roy Hobbs, the mythical rookie baseball player who came out of nowhere to amaze everyone at an advanced age in the classic Robert Redford movie, *The Natural*. Tracy amazed his fellow soldiers at Fort Benning, where he ran circles around his younger comrades, despite being the eldest enlistee at age twenty-four. He, like so many other soldiers, loved life in the army and reenlisted after his first two-year stint ended. A native of Okaloosa, Florida, Tracy was remembered as someone who made friends everywhere he went, and the number of people who attended his funeral easily confirmed this picture. He died of injuries he received on March 17, 2004, when his Bradley Fighting Vehicle flipped over an embankment into a river near Baji, Iraq.

CHAPTER 2

MY EARLY YEARS: THE GIFTS OF MENTORSHIP AND FAMILY

> *If you can talk with crowds and keep your virtue,*
> *Or walk with Kings—nor lose the common touch,*
> *If neither foes nor loving friends can hurt you,*
> *If all men count with you, but none too much;*
> *If you can fill the unforgiving minute*
> *With sixty seconds' worth of distance run,*
> *Yours is the Earth and everything that's in it,*
> *And—which is more—you'll be a Man, my son!*
> —Rudyard Kipling, "If"

My Early Education and Community Involvement

If it is true that life is a series of trials, setbacks, tribulations, and disappointments interrupted by occasional luck and laughter, then perhaps my early desire to serve in the army helped me reconcile the bitter with the sweet. Beginning at the age of five, I swelled with tremendous pride when wearing a uniform, and this feeling would eventually lead me to the U.S. Army. I still have the photographs of myself dressed in my various uniforms from pre-kindergarten through eighth grade. I understood early on that discipline and teamwork would be the hallmarks of my success.

I really enjoyed the leadership roles that I was entrusted within these early years, but I'll be the first to admit that, at this point, I was a better follower than leader. Because I was always the smallest member of my circle of friends, I waited my turn to lead. But when my time came, I used what I had learned in observing those who had lead before me, and I "took no prisoners" on my way to what eventually became one of my real talents—balancing the mission of the military with the need to care for soldiers and their families.

A pattern of personal ambition emerged after these early experiences in leadership, and from then on, I tried to utilize every one of my successes and failures to help strengthen my character. It didn't take long for me to understand that the environment around me would—for better or for worse—have an indelible impact on my future success. As soon as I realized this, I started watching those around me closely, taking their good examples to heart while ignoring the bad elements and generally leaving nothing to chance.

The Cordian Marian nuns that taught me at Christ the King Catholic School were tough and demanding, but my recollection could also be based on the fact that I was not a stellar student and was more mischievous than most. Suffice it to say, I survived this school as a student and an altar boy in large part because of my involvement in the scouting program. I remain convinced that my Catholic elementary education and my involvement in scouting were the keys to my success in my formative years. That combination provided me with many sources of mentorship, which I would probably not have gotten otherwise. I enjoyed my time as a Cub Scout, Boy Scout, and Explorer so much that I became an Eagle Scout at twelve years old, and at the time, I was recognized as the youngest Eagle Scout in San Antonio and Texas. Today, I remain committed to scouting as a member of the Board of Directors of the Alamo Area Council and the Eagle Scout Association and as a commissioner on the west side. I believe in this cause, yet many challenges lie ahead for Hispanic youth, many of whom cannot financially afford to participate in these activities despite their undisputable value.

I was also very fortunate to have participated in the Prospect Hills Yellow Jackets program, which afforded us kids the potential to fulfill our dreams through athletics. Learning from people like Fernando Arellano, his four sons—Fernando Junior, Mario, Lalo, and Robert—and others who had vision and aspirations created a foundation for later efforts in teamwork and helped complement my future professional experiences in the army. I was never the most gifted athlete, due in part to my diminutive stature at that age. But I learned the importance of understanding my role in a team situation and found that greater success is within the reach of those who are willing to set aside their personal needs to achieve a shared goal. That lesson has remained with me throughout the years. After all, each soldier works in a collaborative effort, which reflects his or her impeccable need to be part of the army as a pivotal individual part. Without a doubt, every organization is only as good as the parts, and the Hispanic parts have always played a key role in the success of the army.

I would be remiss if I didn't mention that I also was very fortunate to be part of the Boys and Girls Club of America (although at that time, it was known only as the Boys Club). Here, through boxing, basketball, and other after-school programs, I was able to parlay my other experiences—including my rigorous Catholic education and involvement in scouting programs—with an affordable program that provided additional mentorship and support. My days were full of excitement and fun learning, not to mention guidance from the Boys Club leaders, who shared their values and experiences and showed genuine care and concern for our development as model citizens of the greater San Antonio community. These efforts obviously worked, as those of us involved in the program made it out of the barrio and onto greater success. Some of the notable people who used these valuable experiences to achieve great professional success include Emilio Garza and Edward Prado, both federal judges with the Sixth Court of Appeals in New Orleans, Dickie Peña, past president of the State Bar of Texas, Tessa Martinez Pollack, the president of Our Lady of the Lake University in San Antonio, attorney Robert Arellano, accountant Reuben Escobedo, Robert Elizondo, a former vice president of United Parcel Service, and Charlie Barrett, owner of a successful Jaguar auto dealership. Many others also survived the hardships of the barrio and moved on to a better life, thanks to the guidance and support provided by organizations such as the Boys and Girls Club, Prospect Hill, and scouting programs.

Although it's tempting to dwell on the success of those of us who reached stardom in our professional fields, I often look back and remember those who were less successful but still remain cornerstones of my development when I was young. The lessons that I learned in my old neighborhood remain with me today and guide me at the times when I need it the most. However, I am convinced that education remains the springboard to success; without it, few young people have a prayer in our competitive marketplace. To this day, I believe that if I had not had been so fortunate, I would have ended up falling prey to the scourge of crime and drugs—or worse, I could have ended up dead.

The Importance of Mentoring

The problems currently plaguing the Hispanic-American community were the catalyst that encouraged me to retire from the army after thirty-three years of rewarding service. My parents raised me to value education and the doors it opens for all Americans, regardless of their background, religion, skin color, or financial worth.

Horace Mann—whose name adorns the San Antonio middle school where I attended ninth grade—once noted that "education…beyond all other devices of human origin, is the great equalizer of the conditions of men." That statement retains its power, because it reminds us all that our ability to shape our destiny and improve our lives is dependent most on the commitment we make to our education. I fear that message has passed by a great number of Hispanic Americans. So, in choosing to retire from the army, I was moving on to another battlefront and at the same time answering a calling. From now on, I am a soldier fighting to protect my community in the war against ignorance.

It truly bothers me that not nearly enough successful Hispanics are giving back to their community. Of course, many of us give monetarily, but I believe that face-to-face mentorship is far more important. At-risk youth need to see themselves in us, in order to help them in their personal struggle for a better life. These kids yearn for our guidance—we can give a few dollars here and there, but the thing they thirst for most is our time and attention. The bottom line is that meaningful mentorship with the next generation of Americans is the only thing that will ensure our nation's prosperity and preeminence.

Therefore, as I retired from the army and returned home as a prodigal son of sorts, I wanted to concentrate on community outreach in the west side of San Antonio where I grew up. Although this part of town is now considered part of the inner city of San Antonio due to never-ending urban growth, my focus remains on supporting schools, scouting programs, and the Boys and Girls Club in the area. I serve on the Board of Directors of these organizations, and I am committed to ensuring that local Hispanic kids be engaged in these programs and in the outer community. Moreover, I want to serve as an example and role model to all of the kids in the community. I want them all to realize if someone like me can make it out of the barrio, any of them can, as long as they are willing to live a life of self-discipline and purpose. Scouting programs and the Boys and Girls Club remain perfect fits for young Hispanic youth growing up in these areas, as they offer an array of opportunities and options that may not be available elsewhere. I often use my experiences and successes within these organizations to reach today's youth. The fact that I was an Eagle Scout and that I have been elected to the Boys and Girls Club Hall of Fame gives me entry points with kids that I wouldn't have otherwise. My motivational speeches take me all over the United States, and I continually use these outstanding organizations as springboards to help develop today's youth and the leaders of tomorrow.

I have also formed my own educational foundation to emphasize the importance of education to children in my community and to establish several schools in my old neighborhood that provide these kids with the opportunities they deserve. My recent efforts to assist the Escuela de las Americas by adding the sixth grade to a pre-kindergarten to fifth grade program has offered me a sense of accomplishment that rivals anything I did in the army. The Texas Education Commission has now granted us the opportunity to add a "feeder" middle school, which will be named the General Alfred Valenzuela Leadership Academy. The curriculum will be geared toward at-risk youth who need community involvement, and we will draw from a select list of exceptional role models who will provide the mentorship and friendship that is so vital to these kids. Now more than ever, parents and children can follow a straight path from elementary school to middle school and beyond. The Mexican-American Unity Council, their Board of Directors, and the teachers have done and continue to do untold wonders with these kids every day. They are absolutely awesome, and I feel assured that through our collective efforts, more children from my neighborhood will have the same, if not better, chances to succeed than what I had.

The Importance of Family

For all the time I've devoted to praising the organizations and institutions that were vital to my childhood development, it must be remembered that the successful development of all children begins and ends with the parents at home. I was truly blessed to have a mother and father who were unconditionally devoted to my sisters and me. My father and mother both worked tirelessly to keep us in Catholic school and to allow us to participate in extracurricular activities such as scouting programs, Boys and Girls Clubs, dancing lessons, and sports. We lived modestly, but if we were poor, no one bothered to tell us; truth be told, we were such a happy family that we wouldn't have believed the naysayers anyway. Our house was very small, but it was more than adequate to shelter us all and allow us to grow up in a great—albeit rough—neighborhood. All of this provided me with the essential foundation from which I grew into a man.

I was blessed with parents who toiled all day, often performing several jobs at the courthouse and the juvenile department just to make ends meet and to provide our family with a little bit of security. My father worked hard as a court clerk and used the famous G.I. Bill from his service during World War II to improve his position in life and eventually serve as the first Hispanic court reporter in San Antonio. He educated himself and worked his way up the ladder despite the odds against him. My mother was also an inspiration, steadily making her way through the ranks of the juvenile department in Bexar County, working with kids she didn't even know to help them realize a better life. Both of my parents, at the end of their demanding workdays, came home and provided for our welfare. They faithfully delivered us to and picked us up from the various community, social, and school functions we attended that provided us with better opportunities and a beacon of hope. I now see the pure love that stood behind every one of those colorless tasks, silently expressed and warmly felt. In retrospect, it's obvious that they did the important things right, creating the foundation and strong environment each of us kids needed to become successful in our own individual ways later on.

I was also blessed to be raised in a family in which many of my relatives—a long line of Valenzuelas, Garcias, and Treviños—served their country admirably with total devotion to the future of our nation. From their example, I inherited the belief that freedom wasn't free and was well worth fighting for. Mixed in with that strong work ethic was my family's devotion to contributing positively to the fabric of our community and nation and their belief in service to a greater cause than ourselves, mainly focused on God and country.

The values of my family and friends were abundant and edged on respect, selfless service to others, integrity, pride, loyalty, duty, and personal courage. I was fortunate to receive a great deal of valuable advice from my family on what it took to be a good person and how I should carry myself. I was even luckier to be the eldest grandchild on my mother's side of the family (the Garcias) while also being the first Valenzuela to carry the family name to the other side. My grandparents' steadfast love and focused attention on my development served me well, constantly reminding me of the importance of carrying my families' names with pride and integrity.

The Hispanic community is very family-centric and, as I have shown, provides an important source of support. However, this often works against us, as our focus on family matters too often causes us to ignore other important components of a successful life. Most notably, education is an essential part of the equation of success for Hispanics; without it, we are practically doomed to fall prey to the societal ills that bedevil so many Americans today. At the end of the day, education is something that no one can take away once it is earned. But education is a double-edged sword; the absence of a competitive education serves as life's greatest discriminator.

All of the traits and values I learned in my upbringing helped ease my transition from civilian life to military service. I could never have imagined the wonderful and adventurous path my life would take. God has allowed me to serve in positions and places that I never knew existed before I joined the army. But my most important blessing was being surrounded by the best civilians, soldiers, officers, and noncommissioned officers (NCOs); quite simply, these people are the best that America has to offer. My love affair with soldiering will rest with me forever, and the soldiers who have directly touched the lives of my family and I, in humble yet profound ways, will never be forgotten. The only sadness I encounter today occurs when I recall these experiences and realize that I can't go back and do it all over again.

CHAPTER 3

COMPANY GRADE YEARS: WHERE THE RUBBER MEETS THE ROAD

*We have good corporals and good sergeants and some good lieutenants
and captains, and those are far more important than good generals.*
— William Tecumseh Sherman

Fort Hood, Texas, and Fort Sill, Oklahoma

I was commissioned in 1970 as a distinguished military graduate from St.
Mary's University in San Antonio, Texas. Luckily, my years in the Reserve
Office Training Corps (ROTC) at Jefferson High School in San Antonio
and at the university level, helped prepare me for the rigors of military life
and established a strong foundation for me to master and hone my skills for
the rest of my career in the army. Because my wife Esther was very close to
her family and wanted to stay near our relatives while she was pregnant, I
reported to the First of Sixth Field Artillery, First Armored Division, in Fort
Hood, Texas. This posting was short but very meaningful, as Esther and I
received our first taste of life in the army, and more importantly, our daughter Lori Irene was born.

At this time, the Vietnam conflict was winding down, and many of our
soldiers were in transit, either entering or leaving the army. I was prepared
by the artillery basic course at Fort Sill, Oklahoma, to train and lead soldiers
in peacetime and in war, if necessary. At this time, I performed my duties as

an artillery forward observer, battery fire direction officer, and fire support officer for a ranger company that had just returned from Vietnam. These assignments provided me with important experience for the future challenges I would face. My stay in Oklahoma was cut short, though, as I was selected to attend the helicopter aviation course at Fort Wolters, Texas.

Because of serious injuries I suffered in a helicopter crash at Fort Wolters, I found myself in a different cycle of school and assignments than was normally required for regular army officers. The crash occurred early on in the course, and I then had to report to my next post. Here I was, after one and a half years in the army, and I was hurt and had missed out on part of the normal grooming pattern set forth for officers in the army.

Lessons Learned in Turkey

The real question I faced was whether I could rebound from these unfortunate events and continue on the road to success. To prove my mettle, I volunteered to go to Vietnam. It was 1973, though, and the Artillery Branch was looking for captains with more than one tour under their belts. So instead of going to Vietnam, I was sent to the 528th Artillery Group in Turkey. This turned out to be a very rewarding assignment. I spent thirteen months unaccompanied and separated from my family, working as an artillery advisor for the Turkish army. Fortunately for me, I received a crash course in the Turkish language at the Defense Language Institute (DLI) in Monterrey, California, before I deployed. Although this year away was tough, Esther stayed with her folks, and this turned out to be a great move as our son Freddie was born while I was away. I received the good news that I was a father for the second time through a Red Cross message. Interestingly, the Eighty-second Airborne Division was on a NATO exchange exercise, and through a military affiliate radio (MARS) station I was able to welcome Freddie Junior into our family.

Several things occurred during my time in Turkey that I think were very significant in my development. These occurrences were ones in which my Hispanic lineage helped lead to the final results. Initially, my superiors asked if I spoke Spanish, and I responded affirmatively. I understood Spanish, although my mother and father preferred that we speak English at school and at home simply because both of them had witnessed discrimination firsthand in San Antonio, particularly after the war. Second, I really thought that I could speak Spanish but probably didn't have much command of the language. I headed to California, prepared for a refresher course in Spanish from the DLI. But once I got there, I discovered that personnel command believed—based solely on my answer to their question about my ability to speak Spanish—that if I could speak one foreign language, I probably could pick up another one with relative ease. I still don't completely follow their logic in that decision, but I ended up learning Turkish and was able to take care of myself conversationally during my tour in Turkey.

When I arrived at the command post, I was interviewed for a top secret position in which I was asked many probing questions about my past. After surviving this process, I was made the S2 (intelligence officer) of a command as large as a nuclear delivery brigade, and I had extra duty positions as Equal Opportunity Officer (EOO) and Drug and Alcohol Officer. Because I was the only minority officer, I was the natural choice for advising the commander on racial issues—or so they surmised. Furthermore, the other officers assumed that, because I had grown up in a rather rough neighborhood on the west side of San Antonio, I had probably encountered plenty of drug and alcohol abuse and may have even abused alcohol while I was in college. This was an observation that would have been ill-founded if asked about and was simply made based on what I later learned was a naive perception of my ethnic background.

Return to Fort Hood

After my stint in Turkey, I proceeded back to Fort Hood First Cavalry Division and started on what would be the assignment that would pole vault me past my peers, thanks to my performance in key assignments. Officers such as General Jack Merritt, Lieutenant General John Crosby, Lieutenant General Bill Schneider, Major General Lou Del Rosso, Major General Don Jones, Colonel Homer Gibbs, Colonel Steve MacWillie and their wives really helped Esther and I get to the next level. Even though I was the only Hispanic in the brigade-sized Division Artillery, if not the entire division, their mentorship illustrated sincere caring and assistance based on merit and again provided me with the necessary advice to take on the challenges that arose in my next few years. When I was among these outstanding people, I never felt like an outcast—they didn't care about my background and never made me feel as though I was different.

At this time, the army's system of racial classification was rudimentary at best. When I joined the army, they only had three basic categories for racially classifying their soldiers: black, white, or other. Because I was not black, I was classified as "white" for the first five years until I was rolled into the "other" classification. Still, the army's clumsy attempts at understanding the racial makeup of their soldiers had no effect on my relationship with these exceptional officers. They helped me command two artillery batteries comprised of about one hundred men and also assisted in my development as an assistant S3; battalion S3, in which I was in charge of operations; S4, in which I handled logistics; fire support officer for a division ranger company; and in other important projects within the division.

Several other key events occurred during what would be our longest and only lengthy tour (three and a half years, to be exact) in the army. For one, I was nominated to be a general's aide to Major General Russell Todd. Even though I didn't get this job, I was blessed to have mentors who considered me for such a coveted position.

It is important to note and remember that, at this time, the Vietnam conflict was drawing to a close. Racial and disciplinary issues, along with drug and alcohol abuse, were rampant. In fact, several officers and NCOs were beaten up or killed by their subordinates not only in Fort Hood but also in the army as a whole. These tragic occurrences significantly tarnished the image and reputation of our great army. While on staff duty for the battalion one evening, I was assaulted by three soldiers. Major General Julius Becton, the division commander who later became a Lieutenant General came to the hospital to check on my condition. He promised to take action to bring these men to justice, and this promise was fulfilled, eventually resulting in a general court martial of the three soldiers later the next year. It was gratifying to see justice run its course, but I still had serious concerns about the direction of the army I loved so dearly.

Back to Fort Sill

By the time I arrived at the artillery advance course at Fort Sill, Oklahoma, I was equal to or had moved ahead of my peers simply by the positions I had held at Fort Hood. Luckily for me, I was shortly thereafter selected "below the zone", which is army slang for ahead of my peers, to major. I was the only Hispanic battery commander in the entire First Cavalry Division, and I was the only one of two Hispanic commanding officers on the entire installation at Fort Hood, Texas. The other company commander, Captain Agapito de la Garza, commanded an engineer unit in III Corps. A West Point graduate from Edinburg, Texas, Captain de la Garza was a valuable mentor who didn't allow me to be intimidated by his many accomplishments. He was a great friend to me at this time, and to this day, Agapito, or Pete, remains one of my closest friends. Although I couldn't totally appreciate it at the time, his great peer mentorship was instrumental in my development in this position. I am forever grateful and very proud of him.

Whenever we had a chance to learn from people with greater experience than we, Esther and I did not hesitate to take advantage of the golden opportunity. For example, Esther and I both benefited from the mentorship of Captain Stanley Shipley and his wife Cindy. To this day, we celebrate the fond memories we had spending time together as couples and providing mutual support and mentorship to each other. My success as a battery commander is directly attributable to Stan Shipley, a fellow San Antonio native and graduate of West Point and the Wharton School of Business; Lieutenant Steve Steed; and First Sergeant Jackie (Top) Stanfield. Together we led the best battery of the five in the battalion and two of the top batteries out of the twenty-five or so in the Division Artillery. Although I may have had what some referred to as the rehab/knucklehead unit, between myself, Top Stanfield, and Stan Shipley (my executive officer, or XO) we molded and nurtured the unit to greatness. The credit equally goes to my NCOs, who were also directly responsible for the transformation.

Working in field artillery gun batteries gave me the utmost appreciation for the true NCO corps and a better understanding of why they are considered the backbone of the army. If there was a place where our Hispanic impact is truly felt more than anywhere else, it is in the ranks of the noncommissioned officers. Although I didn't realize it at the time, I can now attest that the NCOs as a whole remain the epitome of what the army is all about. My Hispanic NCOs, although small in number, were well-disciplined, tireless workers without peer. Every once in a while, one of them would fail, but those instances were few and far between. Most were returning from Vietnam, and while some had been decorated appropriately, most were not.

I really didn't figure out the award system until I attended the retirement of my brother-in-law Chief Warrant Officer 4 Albert Treviño. Here was a hero who had entered the army immediately after graduating from Burbank High School, began as a private, attained the rank of sergeant in the elite special forces, and went on to Vietnam in the mid-sixties. Following that, he attended rotary wing helicopter school, flew Cobra gun ships, and returned to Vietnam two more times. As a witness to his retirement, I saw many senior officers receive their Legion of Merit medals, field grade officers and senior NCOs their Meritorious Service medals, and warrant officers and junior NCOs their army commendation medals and certificates of achievement. It seemed to me that the prestige level of the award was based largely on the level of seniority that the recipient had achieved. I couldn't help but wonder if we were guilty of discounting the heroism of lower ranked soldiers.

I didn't understand then—and I still do not today—why so many heroic Hispanic soldiers go off to war and fail to be recognized for their outstanding service to the nation. One explanation is that good soldiers do not serve for the recognition and wouldn't ask for it, because courage and meritorious conduct speaks for itself. I still wonder, though, if Hispanic NCOs ever got what they deserved and whether a subtle form of discrimination reared its head when the time for recognition and accolades rolled around. Was our failure to recognize these men and women due to a lack of documentation, or was it simply that no one took the time to give these soldiers their due? Was it because our military was so big and preoccupied with wartime issues that it simply overlooked these people and failed to take care of its own? I have witnessed in my career a number of Hispanic soldiers who have displayed outstanding courage and heroism but never truly received the recognition and reward that they deserved. Hispanics are proportionally the most killed and the most wounded, and in fact, Hispanics have a twenty percent higher chance of dying in combat than non-Hispanics.[3] Yet they are also the least decorated.[4] On the flip side, Hispanic soldiers frequently eschew awards and recognition, focusing solely on the privilege of serving in the United States Army. It's almost as if their lack of ego works against them when the military honors its greatest soldiers.

I would guess that these five short field troop years in my career were instrumental to my future professional successes; in retrospect, I can say that I had fun, worked hard, and got lucky with the right mentors. I learned that the way a soldier performs during the field troop years as a commanding office or NCO makes or breaks the individual's career. Many careers are won or lost at this level. If one makes it through these tough field troop years, it is likely that the average NCO will opt to stay to take care of his or her soldiers. It also signals the halfway point toward retirement, if twenty years is the goal. Simply put, this is the turning point where the rubber meets the road, and the stakes become much higher.

CHAPTER 4

FIELD GRADE YEARS: THE CROSSING POINT

The outstanding officer will continue to be he who attacks with all of his energy and enthusiasm the tasks to which he is assigned and who grows in stature and understanding with his years and with his experience. Responsibility comes to him who seeks responsibility. It is this officer, regardless of his field of effort, who will be called to high command.
—The Armed Forces Officer (1975)

Climbing the Ladder of Command

The field grade years are key to the development of the young Hispanic officer, because this is the point at which he gets the first crack at serving in positions that ultimately prepare him for battalion and brigade command. Without attaining these two commands, it's virtually impossible and inconceivable for someone to reach the star ranks. In noncommissioned terms, this is equivalent to passing through the sergeant first class, master sergeant, and first sergeant positions, which are all vital in reaching the coveted sergeant major pedestal.

In essence, this is what our job is all about—commanding and furthering the development of some of our society's best and brightest young people. Leading these impressive warriors in times of peace and wartime is an essential part of any successful senior leader's dream. In fact, field grade level officers and NCOs who do not aspire to this type of leadership almost always find it impossible to reach the top echelons of the U.S. Army.

It is imperative for army leadership to realize, however, that not everyone can excel at these command positions. When soldiers are selected for top positions without first taking on tough operative assignments, they falter and many soldiers are cheated of the leadership that they deserve.

Some people, though, even with the right experience, simply cannot lead effectively at this level and, in my opinion, should not be allowed to. The military generally has it right and does a great job of weeding out those who cannot or should not lead. After fifteen promotion boards and four command boards, there is a gut instinct that tells all of us that some officer or NCO just doesn't have the right stuff. Unfortunately, we still make mistakes and allow some people to get to these levels only to find that our soldiers suffer under their inferior leadership.

Today we still have senior officers and NCO leaders who don't command past the brigade level, yet they still get promoted to the next rank. As I've always said, the military owes us nothing and may do as it pleases; however, if the army's leaders believe that the average soldier isn't aware of this problem, they are mistaken. At this critical juncture in our nation's history, we must stand up for what is right. We have standards in the army, and everyone should adhere to them, for failing to do so is ethically, morally, and, in my opinion, legally wrong. The young officers and NCOs cannot be fooled; after all, they are savvy enough to understand the political and personality games that often occur at higher levels. It's one thing when these machinations occur in times of peace. But the stakes are higher in wartime, and it is imperative that our forces operate at maximum efficiency. There is no need to mention names; those who have not truly earned their stripes know who they are. But I remind them that our canny soldiers can see right through them and detect their self-serving modus operandi. What's worse, our army is already in the midst of a retention crisis with its young officers and NCOs. Continuing to promote undeserving senior officers will only hasten the exodus of these fine young soldiers.

Unfortunately, the career trajectory of most Hispanic soldiers ends at the field grade level—the ranks of major, lieutenant colonel, and colonel. In my opinion, Hispanic soldiers are valued most for their tireless work ethic; however, these same soldiers often decline essential command positions and consequently place themselves in a position where they can't compete for the posts that challenge them and give them the greatest opportunity for advancement. As a flag officer recognized as the highest ranking officer of Hispanic heritage in the Department of Defense from 1998 to 2003, I advised senior Hispanic officers and NCOs and told them that they needed to actively seek out leadership positions rather than choosing the easy way out. If there was any area in which I failed miserably as a mentor, it was here. I will always believe that my message was appropriate based on my experiences on promotion and command boards, but not all Hispanic soldiers agreed with my assessment. In retrospect, I may have been imposing my feelings on a different generation of soldiers without adequately considering their perspective, family situation, and experiences.

I would guess that only a quarter of Hispanic NCOs seek the level of education necessary to compete for coveted assignments or to remain in a position of competitiveness. On the NCO side, I believe that there is a cultural component that keeps many Hispanics from seeking more education. Unfortunately, when many of these NCOs are given a choice between enhancing their education to stay in the running for higher positions or staying in the field with their soldiers, too many of us opt for the latter. In short, we are troop leaders first, and we often think collectively to the detriment of our individual career options. If we were to leave the ranks—in other words, if we were to go back to school while on active duty—we would feel like we were cheating the army.

Hispanic officers also face a career trap. If offered an education rather than battalion command, I'm afraid that most of us would rather get our master's degree—assuming that we already have our bachelor's degree. The best example of a program that hurts Hispanic officers, despite its benefits and the benign intent behind it, is the Foreign Area Program. It gives us a chance to pursue a masters and travel; however, in many cases it excludes us from the operations side of the army. This program has proven fatal to many Hispanic officers' budding careers. I don't know how many field grade officers I counseled who were selected for (or could have been selected for) battalion command but chose to get educated and later trained in Central or South America rather than compete for command. In the end, I believe that battalion and brigade command usually proves to be the unkindest cut for potential flag officers. And this problem is not exclusive to the army; there are those in the navy who choose land assignments rather than go to sea duty and those in the air force who opt for ground assignments rather than taking on flying assignments. These individuals also find themselves behind the eight ball at this point in their career.

Is this an ongoing weakness for Hispanic soldiers? Maybe, but we either view getting an education or staying with the troops as the best way to get to the top of our profession. However, sometimes the army as an institution sees these decisions as a way of copping out of the mainstream.

In addition, many Hispanic soldiers enjoy staying close to home and their extended families. This probably isn't as big an issue in today's army, which views families in a more favorable and understanding light. But now we find that many soldiers who have to leave for assignments leave behind their spouses because they want to stay close to home. Ultimately, the soldier ends up going it alone or even volunteers for another unassigned tour. These days, the army has found that more soldiers are willing to go on unaccompanied assignments and risk sacrificing their marriages to their military careers. Unfortunately, many soldiers today cannot envision the future success of their family—with the army as an inseparable partner—in the same light as their successes achieved separate from their family.

Tensions in military families are exacerbated by constant moves, longtime family separation, and the perpetual concerns about the safety and well-being of loved ones. Moreover, military life can be a heavy burden to non-military spouses who wish to maintain their own careers. As a result, divorce and domestic conflict is not uncommon in military families—even more so in times of war. Too many Hispanics abandon their military careers prematurely because they feel too isolated from their spouses and families. This is a tragic development, because the institutional benefits so often outweigh the sacrifices that these families endure.

Very few wives today would put up with the many years in which my wife Esther was alone in raising the kids and leading our family while I focused on my career in the army. While I ticket-punched my assignments, she stayed with our kids and her parents and never asked why I was leaving; in fact, her only question to me was when I was leaving. In hindsight, this arrangement worked for us—but given today's army, our experiences may have been an anomaly. I always believed that I was the one pulling the strings and volunteering, rather than the army moving me, and the accuracy of that belief is debatable. Many officers climbed the same ladder that I climbed at a pace equal to mine or faster without leaving their families as much as I did. In fact, many officers currently in the upper ranks have never been to war, but given Iraq and Afghanistan and the smaller size of our forces, time will catch up with them.

Soldiers see this, but they never complain. Thus, the emerging battle-fronts in our ongoing War on Terror have changed things significantly; now everyone in the army will catch a piece of the action before it's all over.

My Time in Colombia and Korea

My field grade years took me to Colombia, where I worked in the U.S. Embassy during some of the hardest times for that country. The M-19, a terrorist group that is now known as FARC according to many analysts, was terrorizing the country with a ruthless campaign of murders and kidnappings. I was there when they held Ambassador Diego Ascencio hostage for more than seventy days. It was during this tour that I first encountered the so-called "narco-terrorist," a specific type of insurgent who committed unspeakable acts to protect the growth industry of cocaine. Because of my success commanding several artillery batteries and the invaluable mentoring I received from future great generals—including Lieutenant General Bill Schneider, Lieutenant General John Crosby, General Jack Merritt, Major General Lou Del Rosso, and Lieutenant General Julius Becton, among others—I was told by the army that I had made the major list below the zone. Because I was now serving in what turned out to be my secondary area of expertise—foreign area officer—I thought it best to volunteer to go to Korea so that I could quickly get back to the troops.

While awaiting orders to Korea, Esther, the kids, and I attended an embassy picnic. We were just coming off of a whirlwind trip to California for my sister Claudia's wedding, and we were reluctant to attend this function, as we had arrived back in Colombia the previous day and were still battling jet lag and weariness. Despite our fatigue, we attended the picnic, and it turned out to be one of the most memorable days of my life.

While at the outing, we noticed that a canoe holding seven Colombian children had capsized in the cold mountain lake. Although I couldn't explain it at the time, I immediately ran toward the children and dove into the freezing water—clothes and all—to rescue the children. Although I battled hypothermia afterward, I was just relieved that we got there in time to save those children from drowning. Ambassador Tom Boyett later presented me with the Soldiers Medal, which is known as the most prestigious peacetime award for heroism.

Soon after, I reported to the Second Infantry Division Artillery at Camp Stanley in South Korea. Again, I was blessed with a great mentor, Colonel Thomas "J.P." Jones, who later advanced to major general. He took me under his wing and made sure that I got operational credit as brigade S3 and battalion executive officer. Here, I met one of the finest captains, Jose Riojas, who also became a flag officer and the first Hispanic executive officer to be slated as Chief of Staff of the Army. I had nothing to do with his advancement to general officer, but he had an everlasting impact on me. I saw much of myself in him; after all, he was another Hispanic who had transcended tough beginnings with a tireless work ethic and relentless self-discipline. I instantly knew that he was destined for greatness.

Korea proved to be a fast-paced combat arms tour that was right up my alley. But while I was there, I was troubled by the fact that I had left Esther and the kids alone in a new home after I had already spent a lot of time away from them while I was in Colombia.

After Korea, I completed the year in graduate school that I had left before going to Colombia, and Esther, Lori, and Freddie Junior again spent a great year in San Antonio. I'll never forget that night when I called the family to tell them that on my return to the States, we would be headed to the National Security Agency (NSA) at Fort Meade, Maryland. Once there, we were a family again—the kids loved their school, and Esther excelled in her job as a fashion merchandiser.

Intelligence Work

I reported to the NSA and to a small office made up of fourteen brilliant officers, including two more great friends and mentors Sean Maxwell and Colonel Andy Berdy, each of whom were dedicated to a region of the world. My duties included reviewing open intelligence sources and writing papers on issues that could potentially impact our national interests. All of the information I produced in this capacity was subsequently submitted to the army staff. Most soldiers dream of that exact moment in which they can make an important contribution to their country; in that vein, I honestly believe that Major John Bryant and I provided our civilian and military authorities with serious analysis and an important source of proof that

Grenada, a small island in the Caribbean, was being advised by the Cuban government and was intended for use as a satellite for Communist adventurism. We predicted that the Cubans intended to venture onto the island and eventually make it an outpost to further their goal of Communist expansion in the Western Hemisphere. Beyond that, we ended up advising and briefing the army on future engagements in Haiti, Colombia, Panama, Nicaragua, Honduras, and El Salvador. Before the year was up, my job required me to leave my family again in order to be an advisor to the El Salvadoran army.

Advising the El Salvadoran Army

The Farabundo Marti (FMLN), a leftist insurgent group, was engaging the local government, and the U.S. military responded with fifty-five congressionally-mandated advisors to help the El Salvadoran military. Led by Colonel "Smoking" Joe Stringham, my posting called for me to be an infantry/artillery advisor for the Artillery Brigade in San Juan Opico. I was proud to be part of this small, congressionally organized effort. Even though the Iran-Contra events occurred at this time, if it were not for our efforts, Central America, El Salvador, Honduras, and Nicaragua would not be free today from the Soviet-supported, Castro-led, Marxist terrorism. Despite the controversy that our involvement in El Salvador engendered, I remain convinced that our efforts were another success story for the United States in Central America.

It is here that I also met a true friend from the CIA, Felix Rodriguez (alias Max Gomez). Felix's life was deserving of the Hollywood treatment, considering that he helped capture Che Guevara and was also instrumental in saving my life. It was during this assignment that I would be decorated for valor doing what I thought was an act of helping support the real heroes of the democratic process. One night in a small village at San Juan Opico, El Salvador, these great indigenous people braved insurgency and threats of death, standing in mile-long lines for hours day after day in the sweltering heat, making sure they fulfilled their obligatory task as citizens. They had come to vote, and vote they did. At dusk we were attacked, but the El Salvadorian soldiers and I frustrated the insurgents' attempts to deny these people their right to vote. I was honored to be recognized for my efforts, but in my opinion, my acts of valor on that day paled in comparison to those of the brave El Salvadorians who put everything on the line to participate as citizens in a democracy.

Thanks to Felix Rodriguez and soldiers like Sergeant First Class Don Kelly and Master Sergeant Bruce Hazlewood, I am still around to tell this story. In my estimation, they are true American heroes who represent the elite of our nation's fighting forces. They taught me the importance of adding the phrase "plausible deniability" to my personal lexicon in a particularly difficult assignment under extreme conditions in El Salvador. This assignment mingled political, social, and military concerns in a complex way that I had never experienced before. We all promised to keep secret the action that transpired that night without knowing exactly what would come of it. Through their insistence, I would receive the award seventeen years later from General Peter Pace, the southern commander at the time, and eventually the chairman of the Joint Chiefs of Staff.

My Education Continues and Tragedy Strikes

After spending one year in El Salvador, I was selected for a joint school assignment at the Armed Forces Staff College (AFSC). I was selected for this prestigious assignment, even though I had completed the Command and General Staff College (CGSC) by correspondence. The plus was that I had completed the army requirement for mid-level schooling and completed the soon-to-be-required joint credit educational requirement as well. Lucky for me, I received dual joint credit for the AFSC school and my tour in El Salvador. From my perspective, this lucky break would be the first in a nine-year joint service tour across my army career. Because our two kids were well entrenched in school, I would only see my family on the weekends. But thanks to my wife Esther, every visit was special and full of meaning. At this point, I had been separated from our family while in Colombia, Korea, El Salvador, and for six more months in school. My schooling continued when I reported to Fort Sill, with my family following me shortly afterward.

After graduation from the AFSC, and while awaiting orders to go to Pacific Command to be the executive officer for Lieutenant General Bill Schneider, a series of family tragedies struck at home. My father-in-law Albert Treviño suffered a massive stroke while visiting Esther and the children in Maryland. The year 1984 took its toll on our family, as my cousin Raymond and Uncle Stanley died. Worst of all, my beautiful mother-in-law Gertrude "Tulles" Treviño passed away right before Christmas. I battled feelings of helplessness as I continued to work overseas while my family struggled with these losses. Now more than ever, I never felt right being so far away from the ones I loved. How Esther kept everything together in those difficult times still comes off as a miracle many years later. I don't know if her inner strength is attributable to her family, her being a Tejana, or her time in the army with me. Regardless, I am still awestruck by her toughness and perseverance in the face of personal adversity and loss.

After Esther lost her mother, I ended up taking an assignment at Fort Sill, Oklahoma, which also proved to be another outstanding mentoring opportunity at the hand of great leaders, including Major General Eugene Korpal, Brigade General Pete Weyrauch, Brigade General Charlie Hansell, and Colonel Denny Rooney. All of these men helped me along as I moved up the ranks from executive officer of the Field Artillery Training Center (FATC) to secretary general staff and eventually to deputy chief of staff of the Field Artillery School and Center. Both Esther and I grew and were nurtured by the famous "Red Leg" community, which prepared us for my reassignment to the Seventeenth Artillery Brigade part of VII Corps Artillery, in Augsburg, Germany. We were again fortunate to rely on the friendship and guidance of the families of Brigade General Creighton Abrams Jr., Brigade General Lou Del Rosso, and Colonel Ed Anderson. Without their generosity of time and spirit, Esther and I would have been lost.

Battery Command in the Cold War

Starting off as the Seventeenth Brigade executive officer, I moved on to command a unit of the First of the Thirty-sixth Field Artillery Battalion. Although this was one of the largest units in the artillery community, little did I know at the time that their rigid and operations-focused mission essential task list (METL) training was preparing us for the upcoming Gulf War.

The entire VII Corps would eventually head to Kuwait and Iraq, fight the war, and would only return to Germany to retrieve their families, equipment, and belongings before deactivating and returning to the United States. The success of the first Gulf War was another shining moment for the army, and I was blessed with excellent civilian and military leadership on one end and awesome soldiers on the other.

Commanding a battalion, in my opinion, is the epitome of why we come into the army. Battery command of one hundred or more soldiers is a superb experience, but commanding over five hundred soldiers in preparation to take on the Soviets was extra special. Despite all of our planning and training for any eventual conflict, we were all happy to see the Cold War end peacefully with the fall of the Berlin Wall during our tour in Germany. Again, my noncommissioned officers were awesome and led the way. In that regard, they are no different from field grade officers who command battalions and brigades, the senior captains who lead companies and batteries, and the brave lieutenants who lead platoons from the front. They are professionals who are responsible for the day-to-day performance of the soldiers who walk, patrol, engage the enemy, and dominate the key terrain. Our unit, I'm proud to say, was great because of the superb training and focused education system that provides a constant stream of fully qualified and capable leaders. They proved their mettle in the Gulf War by providing incredible leadership that allowed all soldiers to return home safely with no casualties. My pride in our NCOs and their successes in the Gulf War was limitless.

Success in Peru

Already an Air War College graduate, success carried me to the War College after the Gulf War, but again this experience was shortened as I was pulled out of the Inter-American Defense College and was sent to Peru. Like Colombia and El Salvador and their ongoing fight against insurgency, Peru faced a ravishing war of their own against the Tupac Amaru Revolutionary Movement, or MRTA, and Sendero Luminoso (Shining Path). Facing five thousand percent inflation, the widespread killings of innocent people, a cholera epidemic, bombs going off day and night, and the ruthless insurgency, we couldn't help but admire the resiliency of the Peruvian people. I worked with Special Operations folks from both the United States and Peru, along with the State Department to help capture Absimail Guzman and put an end to the bloodshed plaguing Peru.

This tour proved to be demanding on both Esther and my son Freddie, as the conditions were unbelievable at best. Besides having guns in every room, my brother-in-law and recently retired Chief Warrant Officer 4 Albert Treviño came in and served as my son's bodyguard while he went through his senior year of high school. As the U.S. Embassy "drew down" (in other words, returned family members home) because of the threat, I was allowed to keep my family with me, mainly because Esther also worked at the embassy. Two years quickly went by, and working with General George Joulwan and the SOUTHcom headquarters located in Quarry Heights, Panama would be the best preparation for my future assignment as the SOUTHcom deputy commander in chief (DCINC) after it moved to Miami.

Another highlight of my career occurred in Peru, when I met Dick Meadows. Dick is one of the first people who comes to mind when I think of the true and awesome warriors I have met in my lifetime. For classified reasons, I cannot articulate exactly why Dick's friendship was so special to me, my brother-in-law, and the U.S. government, but he was the epitome of the soldier's soldier, as well as a trusted friend and an indispensable ally in our ongoing fight against terrorism and insurgency. Special Operations support from General Wayne Downing and Brigadier Generals Dave Grange and Dale Dailey was also crucial to our success in Peru.

Military Assistance Advisory and U.S. Army South

Following my tour as chief of the Military Assistance Advisory group, I was selected to the Divarty commander of the Tenth Mountain Division at Fort Drum, New York. An absolutely great command tour in the North Country, Somalia, and Haiti, my experience in this position was marred only by a verbally abusive commander who was in love with himself at the expense of others. How he was selected to be a division commander, much less a general officer, is a mystery to me. Despite his poor leadership, ninety percent of his colonels went on to make flag officer rank. We had a great division that was honored time and again for deployments, war fighting, enlistments, and the complete package of soldiering and training. It's a shame that our commander missed the best part of his command by being so selfish with his time, leadership, and mentorship.

Later on, as Commanding General of U.S. Army South (U.S.ARSO) I enjoyed the luxury of commanding troops located in the Caribbean and Central and South America. While I served as a Component Commander, I again had the displeasure of working with a negligent senior commander—a four-star general, no less—who never bothered to visit our troops. His primary responsibility was to them, and I was amazed at his audacity in failing to recognize our soldiers' talents, tireless efforts, and steadfast devotion to the army. He abandoned these soldiers and, due to his selfishness, lost out on the best part of command. Shame on him for forgetting the most important lesson any general officer can learn, that our soldiers are the backbone of our institution and the only reason for our institution's enduring success. He talked a good game, but to our soldiers, he was an empty suit offering nothing but broken promises. Sadly, his failures and deficiencies were not lost on our soldiers.

After a successful command tour, I was sought out by General Barry McCaffrey, General Wesley Clark and Lieutenant General Lawson Magruder to report to Panama and to be the U.S. Army South deputy commander for operations. Normally a brigadier general slot, I was now filling it as a former brigade commander colonel. Once again, this was a short-lived assignment; however, it prepared me for not only the U.S. SOUTHCom deputy commander job but also my eventual U.S. Army South (U.S.ARSO) command position.

The time I spent in the company grade ranks was a true blessing in my army career. I was rewarded with exemplary junior officers and NCOs, and together we had fun and drove onward to success. No doubt, these thirteen years of soldiering gave me what I needed to make general. If my career had ended at this level, I would have been forever grateful to those who helped me along the way. I'm convinced that most Hispanic soldiers truly make their mark on the army at this point in their career, and as a result, they probably enjoy this time the most. This is the essence of what I call the love affair with soldiering, and the passion a soldier feels lingers for the rest of his or her life.

In my thirty-three-year career, both Esther and I have gone on record as enjoying these years the most. As I've told many young soldiers, it is not necessary to make command sergeant major or general to embark on our adventure of professional success; after all, this is what the army is all about, and this is the point where we make our mark on society and history. Enjoying these years helps cement the important lesson that a soldier's destiny of success is not measured by promotions or getting to the top; instead, destiny is delivered by serving with the best and the brightest that America has to offer. Simply put, this is why we serve, and because of this, our mark on history is assured by the contributions we make during these years.

CHAPTER 5

FLAG OFFICER YEARS: THE ROAD TO THE STARS AND ADVICE FOR FUTURE GENERATIONS

The human element pervades all levels of military service. Further, as officers advance in rank they become more complex and sophisticate— personally and professionally—because they are the sum of their experiences in the lower grades as they progress upward.
— Major General Aubrey "Red" Newman (retired)

Serving in the U.S. Army South

While serving as Deputy Commander of U.S. Army South under Lieutenant General Lawson Magruder, I was selected to the rank of brigadier general. Once again, under the tutelage of Generals Barry McCaffrey, Wesley Clark (both SOUTHCom commanders), and Lieutenant General Magruder, I was executing commander policy down range in the area of operation (AOR) with the armies of South and Central America and the Caribbean. Esther and I had just left the cold North Country and the Tenth Mountain Division, and now we found ourselves in beautiful Panama. Although we were returning to the Panama Canal and the military bases back to the Panamanians, we were fortunate to live on Fort Amador and Fort Clayton before the turnover.

The job was a test of my language and my ability to understand the culture, history, and politics of each of the thirty-one countries in this region.

But dealing with the senior military officials and improving our foreign policy through our interaction with the countries' armies was very rewarding. As an extension of the southern commander, I was promoting unity among their military and police forces, military subordination to civilian authority in civil-military relations, the democratization process, and transformation of their armies to better support their national strategic goals.

There is no doubt in my mind that my Hispanic heritage and my fluency in Spanish led General McCaffrey to choose me to go to SOUTHCom, which is certainly not the normal route to the flag officer ranks, especially when one sees other former brigade commanders moving to positions such as executive officer to the Secretary of the Army, Chief of Staff of the Army, and other four-star officer support positions. Could others have gone to Panama instead of me? Absolutely! However, destiny and fate play a role in everything we do, and I remain convinced that my heritage and language were essential to improving things in the SOUTHCom AOR. I'm also convinced that my experiences in brigade command left me with a very competitive record that probably tilted the scales even more in my favor. In return, I truly enjoyed the best of both worlds: I spoke the language, knew the cultures within the AOR, received an education in diplomacy and interagency operations, and received world-class mentorship to boot. To me, reaching the flag officer rank was a twofer, and the army was getting a seasoned combat arms officer and a senior foreign area officer (FAO) in return.

Besides the commanders in chief (CINCs) mentioned above, I had the luxury of serving under the tutelage of previous CINCs, like the Galvins, Woerners, Thurmans, and Joulwans. All had a tremendous impact on my future in the SOUTHcom arena, but none of them affected me to the degree that General Charlie Wilhelm and his wife Valerie did. Although considered an economy of force AOR dominated by Latin American armies, each and every CINC brought something different to the table. The then Chief of Staff of the Army, General Denny Riemer, blessed my career by making me the first army DCINC ever and gave me a chance of a lifetime to work for the first Marine CINC. But never have I known a more sincere and genuine flag officer than Charlie Wilhelm. A true warrior, he exhibited the utmost compassion and understanding of the people he worked with in the Americas, and his confidence in us resulted in a team that continually triumphed in the region. Most army general officers (GOs) didn't hold him in high regard because he frequently demanded the army share of its Title X responsibilities; however, I was honored to be his point man in ensuring that his vision for our force was satisfied. I base my assessment of his success on what my Latin American military brethren told me—that he took the time to understand the countries and their concerns and, as a result, they always knew that he placed their interests on equal footing with the interests of the United States.

Lessons Learned in My Flag Officer Years

Throughout my career in the army, I frequently adhered to the philosophy that I shouldn't press too hard in pursuing my preferred career niche. I was eager to please my superiors, and I believed that the best way to stay in their good graces was to sacrifice my personal goals and needs for what I believed was the army's greater mission. On numerous occasions, mentors asked me why I never moved where my family and I would be the happiest. They argued that the "big break" that I was seeking was just as likely to arise in a location where my family truly belonged. Unfortunately, the wisdom of my mentors didn't really sink in until late in my career. As a result, I ended up placing my family's happiness in a position of low priority in my career plans.

The lesson to be learned from this is that the officer who longs mainly for the sweet smell of success and identifies success only by promotions and prestige, excluding all those other things that make life truly satisfying, ends up keeping his nose so close to the ground that he is unlikely to ever see the stars. Generalship, in its essence, requires a wide knowledge of human affairs, character, compassion, and a never-ending commitment to the development of subsequent generations of young men and women who chose military service as their career. This comprehensive understanding of the human condition is the key element for success in the star ranks—no other aptitude or responsibility can possibly overshadow the importance of knowing how to relate effectively with others. The proud few who make it to the top must have multi-faceted personalities with uncommon skill in interpersonal relationships and a broad understanding of a variety of activities. In order to have a real effect on the men and women they lead, generals must understand what makes people tick. Without this understanding, a general will never command the respect he or she needs to be a truly exceptional leader of soldiers.

The army also prepares aspiring generals for the challenges of leadership at its famous, compulsory "charm schools." In these classes, officers are prepared for the expectations that will be placed on them as they reach the higher ranks. There are a number of important lessons that I took away from these courses, including: (1) the inevitability of change and the importance of adapting to it; (2) the importance of maintaining my reputation and the legacy of the military in the face of myriad pressures; (3) the fact that, as leaders of this military, we are on display at all times and are accordingly expected to provide the best possible example for others; (4) the value of maintaining balance and keeping my priorities in order; (5) the significance of teaching, coaching, and mentoring in career development and the value of leading from the front; (6) the importance of getting in touch with that inner jerk and working on losing the uglier elements in my personality (which usually requires spousal help); and (7) the fact that the army owes us nothing and, as such, the worth of finding a life that is mine outside of the military. The charm school provided all its students with important life lessons that are applicable both in and out of uniform. I credit this course with much of my success in the flag officer ranks; in fact, without the constant reminders of the importance of humility and their emphasis on being people-oriented, I know that I wouldn't have been effective as I was in my last few years in the military.

Challenges to Advancing in the Flag Officer Ranks

I never entered the pantheon of the three- and four-star ranks, and I am convinced that this arena of the institution will remain a tough nut to crack for minority aspirants, especially Hispanics. Despite the great efforts expended by folks like former Secretary of the Army Louis Caldera, General Eric Shinseki, and many others, and the significant strides that have been accomplished, the current group of generals is almost entirely white. To reach the heights where we can honestly say that the army mirrors the demographic makeup of the United States is virtually impossible; the statistics will never allow it.

I believe that the current inequities exist not because of invidious discrimination, but due to the fact that in 232 years of soldiering, those of us in the military never stopped to think about our demographic and cultural makeup and the importance of representing all Americans. In the past, we simply didn't stop to consider whether all ethnic groups were represented across the board. Most of us were concerned solely with serving our country in peace and war, and the ethnic diversity of the force was rarely discussed. Minority and female applicants answered the call and soldiered on, never paying much attention to the future impact they would have on the makeup of the force. I suspect that many of us didn't want to project what the future force would look like, because we didn't want to be treated differently. Many of us also wanted to avoid stigmatizing ourselves with those who believed that our minority status gave us special advantages within the institution. Most people in leadership positions within the military acknowledge diversity problems, but most of them believe that these issues are better handled by others who possess more experience and expertise in these matters. In short, the army is content to let someone else worry about these problems. This is a defensible view from the inside, but to those looking in from the outside, perceptions easily arise that minority officers at the company and field grade levels don't stand a chance to reach the highest ranks—and this observation remains strong in the eyes of the beholder.

It is nearly impossible for a Hispanic colonel to make general in the active force; yet it has happened to at least nineteen of us in the 232-year history of the army. We currently have one retired four-star (General Dick Cavazos of Kingsville, Texas), two three-stars (Lieutenant General Mark Cisneros of Premont, Texas, and the recently retired Ricardo Sanchez of Rio Grande City), and numerous two- and one-star generals. The recipe for success of minorities seeking to join the flag officer ranks includes a tireless work ethic, willingness to act when opportunities present themselves, and the ability to go beyond the call of duty to take on the most challenging assignments that no one else wants to do. It also requires a commitment to accept mentorship and to recognize the invaluable role it plays in career development.

If it is an accurate comparison that the four-star generals represent the board of directors of the army as a corporation, then it doesn't hurt for soldiers to know the board and have them fight for their services when the need arises. These are the senior leaders of the institution, and individuals must share their vision and aspirations for the future direction of the army. Hispanics just need to be persistent to break through to the highest possible levels on their journey up the command ladder. A soldier can be a great staff officer and write and brief staff papers, but he ultimately proves his mettle as a commander. Command is by far the most important rung in the ladder.

Many Hispanics are content to follow and simply do not care to lead at the lieutenant colonel, colonel, senior officer, or senior noncommissioned officer levels; thus, they beg out of the race before it ever begins and make the pool to draw from even smaller. Mentors play an important role in developing an officer's leadership skills, but at the end of the day, that person must take ownership of his career and put himself in a position to compete. Peer ratings are very important, because officers are also judged not only on character and reputation by their senior leaders but also by the way their peers respond to their leadership. However, there are no checks and balances for a soldier to prove his leadership abilities if he has burned some bridges within the general officer corps due to a reputation for speaking up and rattling the proverbial cage. If he stands up for his morals and believes that he has no choice but to say something that goes against the grain, it should come as no surprise that some of his fellow peers may object to his comments. Although the preservation of integrity within the military is valued above all else, I am convinced that some people don't play the game as it was meant to be played. Others say that it becomes a personality contest, and sometimes I agreed with this assessment.

The vetting process along the way is brutal, but it's doable—and it's the only way to get ahead. If the army solicits an individual for whom she is, then that person must be very careful not to do anything to disrupt the military's party line. If a soldier is asked for her comments, she may express her feelings or opinions, but anything she says must be measured and delicately diplomatic. A careless comment made to a friend—or even worse, to the media—could easily come back to haunt the soldier later on. The Inspector General's Office works tirelessly to keep the army purged of those who violate rules or bring shame to the institution. We take care of our own, but we demand that all soldiers demonstrate impeccable personal integrity, character, and devotion to duty. And despite the loyalty we show to one another, we do not tolerate behavior that falls short of the ideals the army has come to represent. Some would say that officers are guilty until proven innocent, and that perceptions, rumors, and innuendo drive the train toward a Star Chamber mentality; however, this is the army's way of ensuring that the nation gets the best and the brightest senior level officers to lead this institution. Officers who do not fit this mold will not be nominated to civilian authorities for further promotions and command simply because we guard our military's reputation and would not embarrass ourselves with a nomination that will hurt the people's view of the U.S. Army. This becomes even more important the higher up we go, because certain senior leader positions require Senate confirmation, which is the ultimate seal of approval. Recently, we added an additional step that requires the secretary of defense to interview numerous candidates before the nomination to the president is even contemplated.

The army's subjective methods for determining advancement of its soldiers remain in place because they have worked for so long and because the army has a vested interest in protecting its institutional autonomy. It can use its own checks and balances, perpetuate its ideals through stringent selection of like-minded soldiers, and create and maintain a dominant, apolitical philosophy. Yet, here again in the Hispanic culture, the ability to speak English, the attainment of a quality education, and valuable mentorship converges to determine the Hispanic soldier's likelihood of success. It is fundamentally important not only to perform well, regardless of the judge's subjective analysis of the performance, but also to develop network contacts that can positively influence the soldier's trajectory into a successful and lengthy career.

Because the military remains bigger than any one group within it, conformity will dictate who advances and who stays in their place. Those that question each facet of the military's policy and continually relate it back to the decisions of the president, the secretary of defense, or our armed forces, will eventually find themselves left out in the cold, thanks to our administration's unfortunate tendency to treat contrary views with skepticism and occasional contempt. In the end, the struggle of Hispanic soldiers to maintain their value within the military and to seek greater reward for their service must transcend everyday politics. Our ambitions are greater and more important than any political party or election cycle, and we must show that our occasional criticisms of institutional policy are grounded in good faith and in the interest of the long-term success of the army.

Theory of Visibility

Throughout every officer's fledgling career, he or she is constantly reminded that their career trajectory is dependent solely on their level of performance in the tasks that they are given. But while performance is the critical standard of a candidate's acceptability into the large pool of peers from which the elite will emerge, its influence becomes much smaller on that candidate's chances for promotion further within the flag officer ranks. Suddenly, performance is just another factor and elements that largely stand outside of an individual's sphere of influence are fair game for consideration. This is not to say that one's success within the flag officer ranks is attributable solely to luck. Just as every person's individual achievements are partially attributable to those people who guided and influenced us in the past, each flag officer will honestly admit that luck was an essential ingredient in their recipe for success at this level.

At this level, the theory of visibility also comes into play in each officer's chances for promotion; that is, the extent to which a soldier has developed contacts and alliances with his peers and superiors influences his further mobility within the military. In other words, the proverbial tree falling in the forest applies to those aspiring to the flag officer ranks. After all, if someone is an effective leader within the military, but the so-called "right" people are not made aware of his or her achievements, this person doesn't have a prayer for advancement.

My own experiences and research in this area illustrates the impact visibility has on our system of civil control of the military. The senior leaders of the military enjoy a high degree of autonomy in selecting future leaders. The four-star generals operate much like a board of directors, and their access to the elite nucleus of officers who survive the rigorous promotion system has historically been dependent on visibility within the military (that is, until the secretary of defense recently took over the reins and somewhat stifled the process). By the time Congress—or more precisely, the Senate—is able to exercise their vote of approval or disapproval over this elite group of officers, the internal promotion system has already pre-selected the soldiers in which it has the greatest amount of confidence. This system has allowed the military to continually choose the officers who most closely represent the military values that were held by the preceding leaders.

Samuel Huntington in *The Soldier and the State*[5] and Morris Janowitz in *The Professional Soldier*[6] both explore the military's need for autonomy, its standards for evaluating officer performance, and how all of this relates to civilian control of the military. While both authors acknowledge that the interrelationship between these values is complex and difficult to analyze, everything boils down to seven independent variables that influence a soldier's opportunity for advancement: (1) seniority; (2) source of commission;

(3) officer/NCO efficiency reports; (4) performance and potential; (5) job assignments; (6) luck and chance; and (7) the key element to success, visibility relating both to the position occupied and the contacts established.[7]

The higher one goes, the less performance figures into the equation as a deciding factor, because one is simply expected to do well at this level. The simple fact is that every soldier who receives consideration for these elite levels has performance reviews and intangible assets that "go off the charts" and often work as a self-fulfilling prophecy. As a result, the decision makers have to consult a whole new set of factors in choosing who will be the next leaders of the military.

Thus, visibility is the factor that most affects a candidate's chances of success and advancement. Early on in the screening process, certain high visibility billets are accorded greater weight on the candidate's report card. At the middle levels, the scrutiny becomes more strenuous, as the initial screening processes have already separated the elite soldiers from the rest of the pack. At this point, a number of other influences affect the fortunes of each candidate, including the opinions and endorsements of superiors, the "good old boy" network, other associations, and personality contests. Any one of these factors could further sort out the remaining candidates. In the end, the cumulative traits of billets and visibility militate against simple chance in the latter stages of the officer's career. As a result, the army's dependence on visibility as a factor for choosing their next group of leaders virtually guarantees that most Hispanic soldiers are disqualified from competition before they even vie for these opportunities. Because so many Hispanic soldiers continue to serve loyally and dutifully—yet anonymously—they exist and operate largely outside the military's radar. Plenty of the blame for this problem lies with the soldier, who suffers at the hand of his or her own passivity and humility. But the military must develop a way to ensure that some of its most talented and valuable soldiers are not locked out of positions they could excel in, based on the visibility problem.

Dealing with Discrimination

In addition to the visibility problem, I feel it is necessary to discuss the hurdles that Hispanic-American soldiers may face in the form of discrimination during their climb up the ladder of command. Despite the fact that the army generally operates as a meritocracy, or leadership by an elite group who are chosen on the basis of their abilities of accomplishments, I have endured a handful of experiences in which a peer has made disparaging remarks to me on the basis of my race. I must emphasize that the vast majority of men and women in the army are decent, charitable people who exemplify the tolerance and colorblindness that Dr. Martin Luther King Jr. envisioned for America, and I am fortunate not to have experienced the outright discrimination that my father, a WWII veteran, and his ancestors endured. However, I feel that the small number of instances in which I experienced intolerance—as a flag officer, no less—warrant a mention, if for no other reason to remind us all to be vigilant against racism and more passive forms of bigotry. I'm not interested in naming names or poisoning the well for the Hispanic soldiers who still faithfully put on the uniform, day after day. But I confess that I am concerned, knowing that some of the guilty parties remain in positions of power and influence in our great military. In my experience, these characters tend to focus not on the well-being of the soldiers entrusted to their care; instead, they occupy themselves primarily with thoughts and worries about where the next star is coming from.

The first incident occurred when I made it onto the two-star list at the one-year mark. I received plenty of words of encouragement and congratulations from my peers, and their praise and approval meant the world to me. However, one call I received stood out for all the wrong reasons. When this person called me, I quickly realized that he didn't know me and had never called me before. His insincerity became more and more apparent as our conversation continued, and I soon understood that he was simply signaling to me that he was concerned that I had gotten ahead of him on the career ladder. While some may find this encounter to be insignificant or subject to misinterpretation, a number of soldiers have described similar occurrences in which an overzealous career soldier fails to mask his disappointment at the success of a minority soldier. Today, this officer serves as a three-star general, without ever having been selected to command at the two-star level. Interesting! During my time there were several others, and they too know who they are.

Another incident occurred after I relieved a Brigade Commander for cause. This well-liked, fast-moving colonel was accused of sexual harassment, and as DCINC, I became the adjudicator for the CINC. Not long after I took action, my peer review ratings took a noticeable dip. If I could trace the source of those less than favorable reviews, I am almost completely certain that it amounted to a retaliatory act by a faction who resented me for enforcing the rules against one of their buddies.

Simply put, these shadowy individuals acted vindictively against me, because I was a threat to their "good old boy" network. I live in peace, however, knowing that I acted to protect the military and our valuable female soldiers from unwanted, unprofessional advances. The accused party received the due process that he was entitled to, and in the end, I made my decision based on a credible investigation done by subordinate general officers. If this protective society of officers feels that it's more important to insulate their members from accountability for their actions, that's their prerogative. But this belief will have no positive impact on the health of our military.

Another instance took place not long after Louis Caldera became the new Secretary of the Army. At that time, I was the senior officer of Hispanic heritage in the Department of Defense. Secretary Caldera, another Hispanic, and the CSA asked for my help in improving the army's record on diversity of the force, minority recruitment, and retention in the army. It was an honor to have been chosen to serve in this capacity, but my selection must have raised some eyebrows in the Pentagon. Secretary Caldera was adamant on seeing more Hispanic officers promoted in the army, and I became bitterly aware of skepticism and resentment among other officers when one of my peers stationed in the Pentagon speculated to me that I was on the fast track for promotion based on the fact that I was Hispanic. He further pointed out that he considered fluency in the Spanish language to be a prerequisite for career advancement in the military, thanks to the fact that the Secretary of the Army was Hispanic. I do not wish to reveal the identity of this fellow officer, in part because he had intimated to me in the past that he loved and respected Hispanic soldiers and their devotion to service. But his comments were still borne of ignorance, and I think they were made in part to keep me aware of my place in the pecking order of seniority. In the end, I believe that Secretary Caldera's efforts were well-intentioned and indeed necessary. I believe, though, that these efforts had an unintended damaging effect on my future advancement opportunities, due to the perceptions of favoritism that other officers held in light of the initiative. The general and chief architect of this movement is a four-star general currently serving in command.

Finally, several senior mentors whom I had relied on for guidance gave me some advice that took me aback when they uttered it. They informed me that in order to go far within the military, it was imperative that I (1) do not speak or let others know that I speak Spanish; (2) do not become an FAO, nor allow myself to be assigned to the SOUTHCom AOR; and (3) do not claim to be Hispanic on my officer record brief (ORB) but instead opt to be counted as "white" or "other" when racially classified.

Coincidentally, they were unaware that the Hispanic category had not been available on the ORB until just recently; moreover, I had already counted myself as "white" and "other" on prior occasions. This advice turned out to be misguided, as I later elevated up to the flag officer ranks and was put in FAO positions of trust and in the SOUTHCom AOR based in large part on my ability to speak Spanish. Considering my experiences, I would never mentor any aspiring officer—regardless of their background—to conceal their heritage in order to get ahead in their career. In order to lead effectively, Hispanic soldiers must remain true to who they are.

This nation needs FAOs who know and understand other cultures, can speak foreign languages, and can relate to other armies, regardless of race or descent. Every ambitious officer must understand, though, that these types of assignments decrease a soldier's promotion potential, because they take him outside the mainstream of combat operations positions. I was the anomaly and enjoyed the best of both worlds. But my experience was rare then, and it is still rare today. Simply put, it is highly unlikely to have your cake and eat it too in the course of a career in the army.

As I put the finishing touches on this chapter, I watched Lieutenant General Ricardo Sanchez retire after being passed over for four-star command. A faithful and tireless soldier for thirty-three years, Sanchez followed me as the senior officer of Hispanic heritage and distinguished himself throughout his career, most notably when he was chosen to lead the American war effort in Iraq in 2003. Conventional wisdom holds that his period of leadership was indelibly marred by the Abu Ghraib prison abuse scandal that erupted in the spring of 2004. However, it is now clear that Lieutenant General Sanchez had committed no misconduct, and the only condemnation pointed at him was that he was not fully aware of what was going on during his command. But frankly, this is a charge that could be leveled against almost any flag officer when the fog of war is at its thickest.

Early on, it became apparent to me that he would not be nominated for his fourth star simply because he would have to go before the Senate to be confirmed. I asked myself some questions during this period, knowing that other senior officers have been nominated under worse conditions, and some of them were assisted by politically savvy senior officers who aggressively lobbied senators to ensure that their hand-picked protégé was selected. These nominees found themselves in a similar situation to Sanchez's, but because the army refused to allow the customary civilian authorities to dictate who would lead their military, the senior officers dug in their heels and continued to support "their boy."

Again, I feel that I do not need to specifically mention names; but rest assured, that one senior officer was put before the Senate several times without hesitation. Why wasn't Lieutenant General Sanchez offered this opportunity to defend himself? As I recall, another senior officer took the Fifth Amendment rather than answer questions as to what occurred at Abu Ghraib. Yet he could have spared the collective reputation of our enlisted soldiers, not to mention the reputation and career of Gen. Sanchez, if he had only answered these questions openly and honestly.

I grappled with many questions as I watched Lieutenant General Sanchez's career abruptly end. Why was Sanchez singled out? Granted, as the senior military officer in Iraq, he was expected to know everything that occurred in his theater of operations, and the Abu Ghraib scandal was a disturbing occurrence that became even more upsetting when the incriminating pictures made their way to television and the Internet. Given that, why exactly did the Senate's support evaporate? Was it simply the alarming nature of the scandal, or did race enter into the equation? Did the Senate punish him for what he did or didn't say or what he did or didn't know? Did Sanchez suffer because he lacked the political connections with the requisite senior leaders in the army and the DOD? Or did he lose simply because somebody had to be the fall guy, and he was the most convenient candidate? I have my theories and conclusions, but I will leave you to judge for yourself.

With Lieutenant General Sanchez, the army had the chance to promote only the second four-star general of Hispanic heritage in the 232-year history of the military. The first was Richard E. Cavazos, who achieved the rank of four-star general in 1976. However, the institution chose not to fight the political system in order to support the best officer for the job. Did the army give up on him too quickly, thus reducing his future chances? This decision, or perhaps the failure to make one, will be discussed for years to come by soldiers of all stripes and backgrounds, especially Hispanic soldiers.

And make no mistake, the disappointing end of Lieutenant General Sanchez's career will remain in the back of the mind of the next generation of Hispanic soldiers vying for senior positions. They, like the Hispanics who preceded them in this great military, do not ask for special treatment or consider themselves perfect or infallible. Nor do they deny that changes within the military have improved their chances of excelling at the highest levels of military leadership. But the army's failure to "go to the mattresses" for Lieutenant General Sanchez has certainly awakened a sleeping giant in this younger generation of Hispanic servicemen and women. They are watching the military closely to make sure that their careers will be treated with the utmost good faith. If it becomes clear that the leadership will not stand behind them when they need it the most, we may eventually witness an exodus of some of the greatest soldiers the army has ever known. This change may not be dramatic or immediate, but its effects would be dire.

For better or worse, the last chapter to Ricardo Sanchez's military career has been written, and the army's loss will be the civilian world's gain. I have no doubt that this fine soldier will excel in whatever endeavor he seeks out in the future.

Succeeding in the Face of Adversity

The key to overcoming these challenges comes down to a few important elements: mentorship, education, luck, and being careful not to get too far outside the box. Despite the challenges discussed above, I will always believe that any young Hispanic in the army can achieve his or her American dream through hard work, drive, and a love of the institution. After all, if I—a boy born to a poor family in the West Side of San Antonio—could make it this far, anyone else can.

As the old adage says, most leaders are made, and few are born. There are some qualities that are inherited that can make a person a good leader. But many people who do not inherently possess these qualities develop them in the course of their career and utilize them effectively when opportunity appears. If leadership is cultivated by a person's environment, we Hispanics may enjoy a built-in advantage in our families, churches, and peers. However, we must also actively pursue our education and seek guidance from those around us; when we do that, the impact we have on the military can be great.

It is also important that we recognize the people who helped us achieve our successes and try to create and preserve an environment that enables future generations to realize their goals as well. In order to create an endless pool of future leaders who set positive examples for others, we must transfer our personal and professional wisdom to others through mentorship. Most importantly, we must always cherish the support of our families and help guide the military families of future generations.

The Story of Spc. Rodrigo Gonzalez-Garza

Spc. Rodrigo Gonzalez-Garza, one of the first casualties of the war in Iraq.

Taken at Spc. Rodrigo Gonzalez-Garza's funeral in Sabinas Hidalgo, Mexico. From left to right: Major Rich Crusan (PAO), Sgt. Ricardo Gonzalez (Rodrigo's twin brother), me, Pfc. Rolando Gonzalez (the youngest brother), Ssg. Ramiro Gonzalez (the eldest brother), Captain Reggie Salazar (Aide).

Rodrigo proudly served his adopted country as the crew chief of his unit's UH-60 Black Hawk helicopter.

Rodrigo with his older sister, Veronica Valadez. The "alpha and omega" of Rodrigo's life came full circle when Veronica gave birth to a son exactly one year after his death. She named the child Rodrigo.

In Memory of
SP4(P) Rodrigo Gonzalez Garza
6 December 1976 - 25 February 2003

The Soldier's Poem

I was that which others did not want to be.
I went where others feared to go, and did what others
failed to do.
I asked nothing, and reluctantly accepted the thought of
eternal loneliness. . . should I fail.
I have seen the face of terror; felt the stinging cold of
fear; and enjoyed the sweet taste of a moment's love.
I have cried, pained, and hoped. . . but most of all
I have lived times others would say were best forgotten.
At least someday I will be able to say that I was proud of
what I was
. . . a soldier.

Anonymous

This was a flyer that the Gonzalez family gave to me after Rodrigo's funeral.

REMEMBERING OUR HISPANIC MILITARY HEROES

Relaxing with Medal of Honor recipient Jose Mendoza Lopez.

Presenting the flag to the family of WWII Medal of Honor recipient Jose M. Lopez. The Pentagon and the Lopez family asked that I reside over the funeral ceremony.

Fort Sam Houston National Cemetery; taken on the day of Jose Mendoza Lopez's funeral.

Living Medal of Honor winners pay their respects at Jose M. Lopez's funeral at Ft. Sam Houston National Cemetery.

The grave site of my Uncle Claudio, who was killed in Okinawa and buried in the Punchbowl National Cemetery (Oahu, Hawaii).

GENERAL VALENZUELA'S CAREER

Boys & Girls Club Hall of Fame Induction, New York (2000).

Battery Command Team, 1st Battalion 77th Field Artillery; from left, 1SG Jackie "Top" Stanfield, 1LT Stan Shipley, 1LT Steve Steed, and me. (The date on the back of the picture reads 18 Jul 1975).

Speaking to my heroes at a gala of the Alamo Airborne Silver Wings Association.

With Sam Verdeja, friend and publisher of *Hispanic Magazine*, at the 2001 Hispanic Achievement Awards.

Hispanic Heroes; from left, my brother-in-law CW 4 (retired) Albert Treviño (Vietnam veteran), then-Secretary of the Army Louis Caldera, me, and my father (a veteran of World War II).

Participating in a U.S. Army South Command Run.

Commander of Divarty, 10th Mountain Division.

Press interview at Fort Buchanan, Puerto Rico.

Press interview at Fort Sam Houston, San Antonio, Texas.

Celebrating the move of U.S. Army South to Fort Sam Houston in San Antonio with Senator Kay Bailey Hutchison.

My new civilian life; speaking at a tribute for Congressional Medal of Honor recipient Louis R. Rocco.

It all begins with my wife, Esther. Here, we celebrate our 38th wedding anniversary.

Esther and me at a Christmas ball.

The family portrait for Christmas 1995; from left, me, Esther, Lori, and Freddie Jr.

Esther relished every opportunity she had to help serve our soldiers' families.

Here, she brought children into our home for cookies and milk.

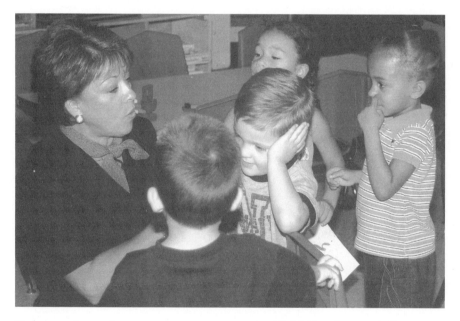

Esther getting to know some youngsters at the Child Development Center in Puerto Rico.

Esther often proved to be a valuable team member around the office, too.

Here, she chats with SOUTHCom commander Charlie Wilhelm and Chairman of the Joint Chiefs of Staff Henry "Hugh" Shelton.

The biggest drawback to the constant travel and moves that my job required was the fact that we were so far away from home and family. As a result, any time we had with our loved ones was cherished.

Here, Esther poses with her brothers and sisters in 1995. From left, Albert, Joe, Mary Jane, Irene, Adam, Arthur, and Esther.

Here I am with my parents and my two sisters, Claudia and Debbie, when I assumed command of the 10th Mountain Division Artillery Brigade at Fort Drum, New York.

My parents remain a source of wisdom and inspiration to me everyday.

Here, Esther and I enjoy a moment with them at the St. Mary's University President's Dinner in 2006.

Now that we're back home and have our grandkids Madison and
Hayden to look after, we enjoy our time with family more than ever.

MENTORS AND FRIENDS

Meeting with LTG Lawson Magruder (left) and Chairman of the Joint Chiefs of Staff John Shalikashvili (center).

Esther and I greet two of my greatest mentors, Chief of Staff of the Army Denny Reimer (center) and SOUTHCom Commander Barry McCaffrey. (far left).

Another fantastic mentor, General (retired) Jack N. Merritt.

Assisting Southern Commander George Joulwan.

LTG Magruder (left), SOUTHCom Commander Wesley Clark (center) and I discuss the matters of the day.

Esther and I hosted Army Chief of Staff and Mrs. Gordon Sullivan for Thanksgiving at Fort Drum.

Consulting with General Peter Pace, who would later become Chairman of the Joint Chiefs of Staff.

Esther and I enjoying a moment with two more great mentors, SOUTHCom Commander Charlie Wilhelm (far right) and his wife Valerie (third from the right). Joining us on the left is the mayor of Coral Gables, Florida, and his wife.

I look on as General Larry R. Ellis, U.S. Army Forces Command Commander, presents Esther with the Secretary of the Army Public Service award for her ongoing support of soldier and family member initiatives.

General Eric Shinseki is a true hero and role model to emulate—a soldier's general.

CHAPTER 6

ESTHER'S STORY: MY ADVENTURE OF A LIFETIME

My parents taught me strength and gave me confidence, but it was the army that gave me my wings. Because I had to make it on my own, I am a stronger woman, and I have a very strong relationship with both of my children. I had the opportunity to give to others, and I have changed lives and learned from many of those whom I helped.

—Esther Valenzuela

I have spent the previous pages giving you a glimpse of my military career through my eyes. I remain proud of my accomplishments in the army, but I couldn't possibly have done this alone. No soldier's success occurs in a vacuum; instead, we all find ourselves indebted to a network of unsung heroes who make all the difference in the world.

Most commonly, soldiers rely on their families as their chief support unit. Spouses, mothers, fathers, sisters, brothers, and children do much more than keep the proverbial home fires burning. They all play a role in helping their soldiers maintain balance and perspective in light of the difficult jobs they must perform. But unfortunately, many of our men and women in uniform cannot rely on this familial advantage. In many cases, these servicemen and women joined the military without a strong family network. Others can sadly attest that divorce and other family misfortunes do not confine themselves only to civilian life. In light of these truths, every soldier I have known will confirm that their family remains the most cherished element in their complicated life.

I am no exception. My personal victories were sweeter because I was able to share most of them with my family. However, these celebrations were not merely instances in which I shared my life out of begrudging obligation. I always believed that Esther and the kids were the most deserving participants in our festivities, because they were all willing and faithful participants in my climb to the top. In short, I couldn't have done any of this without the love and support I received from my wife Esther and my children, Lori and Alfred Anthony (Freddie Junior).

Those familiar with the Book of Esther will remember that she made history by courageously revealing to King Xerxes the plot to destroy her people. Her brave appeal to the king came at great personal risk, since she had carefully concealed her Jewish heritage at her cousin Mordecai's request before she was named queen. My wife would be embarrassed at being compared to this biblical hero, but I still see striking parallels between these two amazing women. Neither of them lost sight of their identity or faith. Both of them were willing to sacrifice themselves to protect the people they cared about. Finally, they both used their eventual positions of influence to help those who were often forgotten in the grand scheme of things.

While one Esther endures as a hero celebrated by Jewish people everywhere, the other remains my hero. She has been my love, my confidante, and my trusted counselor throughout every major challenge that has emerged in my career. This is her story...

Esther

I am often asked what it takes to be the wife of a general. In all honesty, I don't have a stock answer to that question. As with many other challenging but important roles that we take on in life, there's no universal instruction manual that I could refer back to during our adventure in the U.S. Army. Despite this lack of training and preparation, I was fortunate to have a wonderful family and an amazing network of friends to assist me or show me the ropes whenever I needed it. That's not to say that I didn't experience some rough patches along the way. But it didn't take long for me to hit my stride and find my niche as my husband Freddie embarked on his long successful career in the army.

Just as every person is different, every army success story you hear will be a little bit different, too. Our successes were attributable to a number of factors—some of which were out of our control. But, in the end, I believe that my husband's and our family's came about because we never lost sight of each other. The army was the roadmap of our lives, but we never forgot who was in the vehicle.

I wore many different hats in our thirty-three-year adventure. At one time or another, I specialized in protocol, coffees, luncheons, bridge, support and readiness, and volunteer work—including the Red Cross and Army Community Service. My motivation was always borne out of the love I felt for my family.

As I sat in the military aircraft in Laredo, Texas, waiting for my husband, Freddie, to cross the border from Nuevo Laredo, Mexico, where he was eulogizing one of the first soldiers who lost his life in the Iraqi War, I started to reminisce about how I became a general's wife. Although I met Freddie years before, the actual journey began in 1970 when I became a new bride. That is when the adventures of our life together started, and the army quickly became the roadmap for our lives.

In the beginning, I don't think I could ever have imagined the life I would end up leading. I was born in San Antonio on October 19, 1948, to Albert and Gertrude Trevino. I have six siblings: Albert, Joe, Mary Jane, Irene, Adam, and Arthur. I am the youngest, but I was treated like all the rest, and there was no favoritism. Rules were rules, and nothing would change that. Despite the fact that I was born ten years after my first brother, my parents still followed the strict upbringing that they used with him, and they were not too tired after six other children to reprimand or discipline me. Even though my parents had very little monetarily, they instilled in all of us a sense of protocol and respect. My father always sat at the head of the table, and my mother sat at the other end. We did not serve ourselves until after our parents had served themselves. We were expected to always use proper manners, including answering them with the requisite "yes, sir" and "no, ma'am," and we were required to be respectful of anyone who was older.

I lived in a neighborhood that was a mix of Anglos and Mexican Americans. All the kids that lived around us always seemed to congregate at our home, further crowding the nine of us already living in our two-bedroom house. Every day my Mom would cook homemade tortillas, and it always seemed as though children could smell her homemade cooking from blocks away and inevitably ended up at our house for a snack or a meal.

It wasn't until years later that I realized that I grew up poor. I remember eating eggs and gravy in the morning, or what we called huevos perdidos, which translates to "lost eggs." We thought we were eating a lot of eggs, but what we were really eating was lots of gravy with only a few eggs. Feeding seven children each day was costly, but Mom wanted to be sure that we ate some type of warm breakfast before we went to school.

I remember all the other children taking sandwiches to school while we took tortillas with butter for lunch. My brother, Albert, often sold his tortillas for ten cents a piece so that he could buy himself a hot meal. I would never give mine up, because I loved them. I knew Mom had woken up especially early to make the tortillas. Knowing she had taken that type of time to prepare our special lunch precluded me from ever giving mine away or selling them. I still love making homemade tortillas.

At Christmas time, we sat around and played cards including spades, thirty-one, poker, Old Maid, and Go Fish. We never had toys underneath our tree. Mom and Dad could not afford to buy each of us a toy, and if all of the children could not expect a special gift under the tree, none of us were going to get one. We really didn't know that we were missing out, because every family in our neighborhood was going through the same tough times. When I was growing up in the 1950s, we never complained about the toys we got or didn't get.

When I was five years old, we moved from my old house to a home roughly two miles away. We lived across the street from a convent, which later was my elementary school, St. Phillip of Jesus. For the next eight years, I was educated by the nuns who were dressed in black and white from head to toe. Because they stayed on the porch in the evening, they kept a watchful eye on me, even when I didn't want them to. They would look on with concern as they watched me transform into a tomboy who only wanted to play baseball with my brothers.

My volunteer service came every summer. For those three months, I helped clean and prepare the school for the upcoming year. We would wash desks and tidy up classrooms in order to get the school ready for the students that would be attending in the fall.

During the school year, I played softball and became a girl scout. I was lucky because we had the opportunity to have Big Sisters in my scout house.

These ladies came from the Travis Park Lutheran Church, and they gave their time every Tuesday to come mentor us and teach us etiquette and anything else necessary to become a good young citizen. They took us to expensive restaurants to instruct on proper behavior and the safe handling of cutlery. We were able to learn from them that there was a correct order with which to use our utensils. It was only on these special days when I was invited by the Big Sisters that I was able to enjoy these restaurants; my family was not able to afford paying for all of us to eat at any restaurant, much less the expensive ones that I was fortunate to eat in with my Big Sisters. As a result, I learned to savor these Tuesday nights. Eventually, I had to leave the scouts, because it had become too difficult for my dad to drive my sisters and me to our distant meetings. I missed those Tuesdays. However, I quickly learned that leaving the scouts allowed me more free time to pursue my first love—softball. In 1964, I became the Catholic Youth Organization (CYO) Outstanding Athlete of the Year. To this day, I live for that sport.

After eight years of Catholic school, the cost of the private education became too burdensome for my parents. When I began my last year of junior high school, I ended up attending a public institution for the first time. I felt left out at first, watching my friends stay together to continue their private school education. But once I reached junior high, I met a few others who had suffered the same financial hardships. They also had started their formative years in a Catholic school, and, over time, made their way into the public education system. After my year in junior high, I attended Luther Burbank Vocational High School in San Antonio, Texas. Despite the fact that it was a vocational school, it was the only one that was in our district, and therefore, it was mandatory that I attend.

I was an average student in high school. I remained dedicated to softball and became a member of the Orange Jackets, a pep squad that supported all of the athletic organizations. As an Orange Jacket, we drilled, ushered at the Rodeo, and volunteered around the community.

The most memorable event of my high school years was being allowed to start dating. I was allowed to go on one date per month, and I had to be accompanied by a chaperone—usually one of my brothers came with us. I always had a great time, and I experienced none of the pressures that young people contend with in dating nowadays. It was always good, clean fun with lots of laughter and enjoyment. There just isn't much a person can get away with when there are three or four people in a car. I had to sneak around to use the phone, since my father thought it was a waste of time to rehash all the events of the school day, and he would always be concerned an important phone call would come in while I was chatting with my friends.

In the summer after my junior year, my cousin and four other friends attended a quinceañera, the customary coming-out party for a fifteen-year-old female. At that party, we were in different groups. There was a group of girls and a group of six boys. I spied a short guy in the center of the group that generated a lot of attention. Although he was making everybody laugh, I could not help but think that he was a bit cocky. My cousin, Mary Ellen, or Bebe, was laughing along with the boys. I asked her about the group of guys, and she told me that they were all recent graduates of Jefferson High School and future attendees of St. Mary's University. She also told me that the name of the short jokester was Freddie Valenzuela.

Lo and behold, I received a call from the jokester the next day. He expressed interest in my cousin and wanted to get her number. During our phone call, we discussed the events of the previous evening. I asked about the tall, good-looking man with him and was told his name was Robert Arrellano, Freddie's best friend. In exchange for my cousin's number, he agreed to give me Robert's number. We continued to discuss our summer plans. Freddie would be going to summer camp, and he was looking forward to attending St. Mary's because of their outstanding ROTC program. He felt like the program was the ticket to his dream of becoming an officer in the U.S. Army. I remember telling him to look me up in five years, after he had completed school and joined the army, because I would be happy to marry him at that time. What impressed me at that time was his drive and ambition. Compared to the other guys that I had dated, he knew what he wanted for himself and was intently focused on his accomplishments and future plans.

Five years later, Freddie looked me up. Before that phone call, he and I kept in touch periodically. We would call to check up on each other, and a couple of times a year we would see each other or attend one of his university functions. Months would often pass between our conversations or meetings.

Strangely enough, we worked at the same location and didn't even know it. We both had jobs with a small insurance company that would eventually become one of the world's largest insurance companies and banking institutions—the United States Automobile Association (USAA). One day, I was leaving late from work, and he was coming in. We passed each other, and I asked why he was there. He explained that he was working there in the evening for extra cash. He invited me out for a Coke, and we resumed our courtship.

Despite the fact that I had vowed to wed him, over that five-year period there were times when he tested that promise. For instance, about a year after we met, he purchased an engagement ring for me. Not just a ring, but a really nice ring; it was over a carat and had an impressive number of diamonds around the larger diamond. He was working five jobs at the time while attending school and signed over his life to pay for those diamonds.

One weekend during our courtship, I agreed to attend a fraternity party with him at St. Mary's University. He and a number of his fraternity brothers decided that he and I needed to go to Laredo and elope. I quickly understood that his decision to get married was egged on by his buddies and a copious amount of cocktails, and I wisely passed on the invitation but played along with their plans. While Freddie, his four friends, and I were waiting in the car, I convinced the five of them that I needed to stop by my home for some personal items. The moment their car stopped at my house, I jumped out and ran for safety. My father came outside, and Freddie suddenly sobered up. My father made it very clear to him that I had a family. He explained that because I had a mother, a father, and siblings, I deserved a more respectable wedding, and I was not going to cross some border to become his wife. As Freddie backed up toward the car, he let my father know that he understood.

As the saying goes, "If at first you don't succeed, try and try again." Six weeks later, Freddie tried again. This time my mother met him at the door and told him that if he was not man enough to marry me through the Catholic Church, then he was not man enough to marry her baby. I guess it all finally sunk in, because in September 1969, he came and humbly asked my parents to marry me. This time my ring was a little smaller—more like a friendship diamond than the first ring. I eventually asked about that first engagement ring. Freddie proudly let me know that I was sitting in it. He had traded the ring in for a car—a 1966 white Super Sports Chevelle. My, how I hated that car!

On the first of February, 1970, we married at St. Phillip's of Jesus Catholic Church. We had a nice celebration with family and friends. Looking back, I remember the importance of our dollar dance. This is a dance that allows the guests an opportunity to dance with the bride or the groom in exchange for a donation ranging from a dollar and up. In our case, the dollar dance covered our first month's rent. Our first home was a one-bedroom apartment that was previously the maid's quarters of an old Victorian house. It was furnished, so there was no need for me to worry about decorating. Thank goodness, because the fifteen clocks we had received as wedding gifts would not have adequately decorated our first place.

Then the trouble began. After he was commissioned as a second lieutenant in May 1970, we were stationed at Fort Hood, Texas. We moved into a home that had been built before World War II. There were holes in every wall, and the bathroom was equipped with one stand-up shower. This was my first real test as an army wife; I had to make do and learn to be creative with what we had. I hung pictures at every level to hide some of the holes. The mattress caved in the middle, and one of us would have to get up first and help the other out of bed each morning. Although we thought this was a long-term arrangement, we only remained there a few weeks. Shortly thereafter, we went to the field artillery basic course at Fort Sill, Oklahoma.

Soon after we arrived in Oklahoma, we learned that I was pregnant with our daughter, Lori. With my hormones racing at one hundred miles an hour, I was suddenly certain that I had made a mistake by getting married, and I made Freddie's life miserable. Every night around eleven o'clock, Freddie would go and get my banana split. He had the attendant at the local Dairy Queen trained to stay open a little later to allow him to get my nightly dessert. But I will never forget the day before his last exam. I kept telling him that I needed to get home to San Antonio, because I wasn't sure I wanted to be married anymore. Freddie's exam was the next day, and yet we drove over seven hours to get home. When we arrived, my father asked me several questions. "Did your husband beat you?" "Does he give you money?" "Does he put food on the table?" After I answered no to the first question and affirmatively to the rest, it was clear that Freddie had diligently held up his end of our marital covenant. My father told me that I needed to get back in that car and return to my new home. My father also reminded me that he would never hear of a divorce in our family, and that was that. Needless to say, with no sleep and fifteen long hours on the road, Freddie flunked the exam. We stayed six more weeks to complete the course and then returned to Fort Hood.

At Fort Hood, my pregnancy began to take its toll on me. I was suffering from toxemia and high blood pressure. Because Freddie spent countless weeks in the field, we decided that I should head back to San Antonio where I enlisted a civilian doctor, Dr. Margaret Curtis, and my parents to watch over me for the duration of my pregnancy. On January 30, 1971, at three o'clock in the morning, I went into labor. By chance, Freddie had come into town that weekend on leave. At 7:32 a.m., I delivered my first child, Lori Irene. Like most new moms, I was certain that I had delivered the most perfect, beautiful child ever. Six weeks later, I returned to Fort Hood, where we lived on Lockridge Loop, an area specifically for company and field grade officers. Because I was a jittery new mother who didn't know anyone there, much less the child-care and babysitting arrangements available to me, I stayed home all the time with Lori. In fact, for months, other soldiers often asked my husband if he really was married and had a child.

We were First of the Sixth Field Artillery, First Armored Division. Freddie's commander at that time was Lieutenant Colonel Allen Stern. His wife Barbara was very considerate, frequently calling to ask if I needed anything.

From 1972–1973, our small family embarked on a whirlwind of tours, going from Fort Wolters, Texas, for helicopter school to Fort Benning, Georgia, for airborne school to Monterrey, California, where Freddie learned Turkish at the language school. Because Lori was so young, she quickly picked up on various Turkish words and enjoyed secret conversations with her father.

Luckily for me, Lori and I had a lot of time together while Freddie attended his classes. Because the cost of living was so high in California, we could afford to do little. But that didn't stop us from enjoying the beaches of Monterrey and Pacific Grove.

After completing the language school, Freddie was assigned overseas to Turkey. Because his tour was unaccompanied, I went back home to San Antonio to live with my parents while he was in the Middle East. A month after he left, Freddie called from Turkey and wanted to know if I was pregnant. He had been suffering from his own form of morning sickness, including nausea, diarrhea, and vomiting. I had been feeling really well, but I still went to the doctor and was amazed to learn that I was pregnant, just as Freddie had suspected. Since I was living with my parents, I enjoyed the royal treatment. In fact, on many occasions, my dad and I would head to the

Pancake House in the middle of the night while my mom stayed home to care for Lori. Despite the obvious perks of having my parents available, this pregnancy was more difficult than my previous one. In fact, I was ordered to spend many of those days on strict bed rest.

At 6:30 a.m. on November 27, 1973, I was rushed to the hospital with labor pains. Little did I know that I was very ill. My blood pressure was very high, and the doctors were concerned about my immediate future. The doctor came out to tell my mom and my mother-in-law that they were going to have to work on saving just me or saving just my son, as it looked almost impossible that both of us would survive. My mother desperately grabbed the doctor and said, "You cannot force us to make a choice between my daughter and her child. Her husband is not here to help us; please save both of them." At 10:32 a.m., my second child, Fred, was born. I had a high fever and was unable to see him for most of the day. Around 4:30 p.m., I caught my first sight of my child. The stress of the birth had taken its toll on him. He had really red hair and a red face. I was convinced that he was not mine. I kept telling the nurse to look at his armband to be sure that his band said Valenzuela. As it turns out, my mother-in-law had some Irish heritage. Freddie was notified by the Red Cross that he was the proud father of a baby boy, Alfred Anthony Valenzuela II.

Freddie had the opportunity to return to the United States for Christmas. He came home for two weeks to meet our second child. The day after Christmas, when he was scheduled to go back to Turkey, was a heart-wrenching day. Lori kept crying and holding onto Freddie, telling him that he could not leave and go back. She begged him to stay. Lori and I held each other and sobbed at the lonely gate of that airport, heartbroken at the thought of saying goodbye once again. I kept reminding myself that it would only be six more months, and then we would be a family again.

In April of 1974, Freddie returned and announced that he was ready to take his family to Fort Hood again. It was then that everything hit the fan. This was when I was taught about the *real* army. Freddie was with the Divarty, 1st Cavalry Division. He commanded both A Battery and B Battery. This duty station would prove to mold my future. There were so many things that I learned while living at Fort Hood, including the demanding role of a commanding officer's wife, the accompanying oxymoronic "mandatory" volunteering opportunities, and the expectation that I would serve as a role model for other soldiers' wives.

My new role as a military wife was completely new to me. Luckily, I had many wonderful mentors who taught me everything I needed to know to do my part for the army. They first explained to me that as a military wife, my conduct and willingness to serve would have a definite impact on my husband's career and the army as a whole. My mentors included Barbara Schneider, wife of Lieutenant Colonel Bill Schneider, Margie Herring, wife of Lieutenant Colonel Bernie Herring, and Mrs. Fairweather. Despite the fact that I had no knowledge of coffees or the army life in general, they were able to guide me and help me learn the ropes of my new role.

I received my first invitation to a coffee and immediately peppered Freddie with questions. Why coffee? I didn't even like coffee. I had assumed that I was invited to a mere social gathering, where we would drink coffee and engage in small talk. However, my first coffee was unlike anything I had ever imagined. I quickly learned that these coffees were one of the most popular and effective ways for army wives to learn about what was going on around the installation and what we could do to help. As a relatively uninvolved captain's wife, I soon realized that I had no idea what was happening at our installation. I had spent the first four years of our career bouncing from one state to another for short periods of time or riding out my pregnancies at home. Now I was beginning to understand the breadth of responsibility and involvement within the community that was expected of an officer's wife. An ongoing parade of sign up sheets— for bridge, Red Cross, Army Community Service, school activities, and future coffees—circulated around the room at my first coffee. I asked about the sign-up sheets and was told that each sheet represented some organization or opportunity to learn more about the Fort Hood community. Sure enough, the next day the commander's wife called me to be the fourth member of a bridge group that met every Tuesday morning. I had no idea what was going to occur at these gatherings, much less how to actually play bridge. Of the four of us in the group, I was the only captain's wife. All of the other wives were the spouses of higher field grade officers. The pressure was on to make sure I appeared to be adding our scores correctly, playing the right cards, and making sure my conversation was appropriate.

There was a certain dress code and etiquette that we were expected to adhere to. The army taught us to attend luncheons wearing hats and to show up to change of commands with hats and gloves. These customs were eventually phased out, thank goodness. While I enjoyed the camaraderie with the other wives, the dress code seemed excessively formal and old fashioned to me.

Aside from learning about coffees, bridge, and general protocol, I discovered that my most important role as a military wife was teaching other young wives about the "army way" and helping them get their start in a lifestyle that seemed so unnatural to so many of us. Not only was I a mother to my children, but now I was being molded to mentor other young wives and to mother the girls and women that would follow in my footsteps. For example, I remember a sixteen-year old who was living with a soldier. She was still a child and desperately needed my guidance. We arranged for her to be married through the Justice of the Peace so that she could share and enjoy the benefits of being a military wife. We also enrolled her in a local high school so she could obtain her diploma. Other times, when the men were out in the field, a young wife would have a need or a question; as the battery commander's wife, I was expected to assist them in any way that I could.

Even though I had to endure all these stresses, I decided to take a psychology course to learn how to deal with the many issues that accompany childrearing. My children were three years and six months old, and I wanted to figure out what made them tick. Halfway into our duty station, Lori, my baby, started school. It was a heartbreaking, defining moment for me as a mom. Lori and I had grown up together in the army, and now I was letting her go. I remember crying that morning from nine until eleven, when she returned. I couldn't believe how happy she was and how excitedly she expressed her enthusiasm to return to school the next day. I admired how brave and enthusiastic she was about her first day at school; however, I was a little irked that she didn't take a little time out of her busy schedule to pine away for her poor mother.

As Lori and Fred Junior got older, I became more comfortable leaving them at day care. The short time that they spent in day care allowed me to volunteer for Army Community Service. I believed that my willingness to serve would encourage other wives to volunteer. I was always a big believer in leadership by example. After all, most leaders gain more credibility when they show their willingness to do the same things that they expect others to do. If I, as the commander's wife, rolled up my sleeves to get things done, I figured that would prove to the other wives that my endeavors were worthwhile.

Near our fourth year at Fort Hood, Freddie was asked if he would stay and command another battery. I said absolutely not. I knew that Freddie was close to passing the ripe time to go to the advance course. It was necessary to his career that we moved on, regardless of the upheaval that would result. Shortly thereafter, we packed up the kids and our household and moved.

We had amassed quite a collection of cacti while living at Fort Hood. We put them in ammunition boxes as outdoor decoration. I purchased the ammo boxes on sale at the Academy surplus store in Killeen, Texas, where my brother was part owner. Because they were such a great deal, I would buy them whenever new ones came in. The boxes lined our driveway and contained at least 15 different types of cacti. I convinced the movers that, since this was a simple door-to-door move, it would not be difficult to transport the cacti to our next duty station. I begged, pleaded, and offered my undying gratitude to the movers if they would move the cacti and put them around the back of our new house when they arrived and unloaded. They agreed, and a week later they showed up at Fort Sill. To my disappointment, all of the ammo boxes had tipped over in the back of the moving van, and there was dirt everywhere. Everyone who touched things in the moving van had splinters from the cacti. Despite a little blood and a lot of dirt, we enjoyed our lined driveway of cacti once again.

It came as no shock that within six months we had orders to move once again. This time we would return to our hometown of San Antonio. We went there so Freddie could earn his master's degree at St. Mary's University. It was nice being home even though we knew our stay would be short-lived. Upon his completion one year later, we were ordered to move to Bogotá, Colombia. This was our first real big adventure. It was the first time that any of us, except Freddie, had crossed the U.S. border. The night before we were scheduled to leave, the Pentagon called Freddie and informed him that he would be leaving Texas unaccompanied. The M-19, a vicious guerilla organization, had taken twenty-one people in the U.S. ambassador's office as hostages. Entering the country was dangerous to anyone who was unfamiliar with the situation in Colombia and even more dangerous for Americans.

Freddie ended up leaving on his own, and the kids and I joined him in Bogotá two weeks later. Talk about a debacle—we arrived in Miami only to learn that our next flight was cancelled. I had two children, a dog, and enough baggage to live for months. After enduring a six-hour layover in Miami, we arrived in Bogotá and were welcomed by five armed men storming toward us. Needless to say, we were all a little startled by our stern welcome to Colombia. Martial law had been declared due to the insurgent uprising, and the men were from the Colombian army security force, responsible for ensuring our safe entry into our new home. They took each of us individually and rushed us out of the airport in record time.

Going down the Colombian highway at a high rate of speed was frightening. Our vehicle moved silently but purposefully down the highway. The seriousness of the guards underscored the grim state that this country was in. We were taken to a pension, or guest house, where we stayed with three other American families for almost three months. Within two weeks, Freddie was gone. It was up to the other wives and myself to find a secure area for us to live. After we left the pension, we moved into a home that became our personal fortress. It was gated, and armed guards walked by the home twenty-four hours a day. The kids and I had never been exposed to such living standards, and I struggled to adjust to the fact that we were potential targets.

The kids attended an international school, Colegio Nueva Granada. The school was academically superior and turned out to be a challenge for the American students. The school boasted students from only the rich, upper class in Bogotá in addition to the foreign students who attended. It was sobering to walk the kids to the bus stop on their first day of school accompanied by an armed guard. Inside the school bus sat two more guards riding with students. Aware of the dangers, the kidnappings, and the bombings that were going on all around us, I was a nervous wreck every day when I said goodbye to the kids, and they rolled out of my sight.

Just two weeks after the kids enrolled in their new school, Fred Junior came home very ill. His condition worsened the following day, so Lori and I packed him up, and we all took a taxi to the American Embassy so that he could see a doctor. Unfortunately, no doctor was available at the embassy at the time. They told me that I would have to take Fred to a military hospital in the city. The three of us took another taxi and went to a local military hospital. The conditions in this facility were shocking; it was not as clean or orderly as the hospitals we were accustomed to in the United States. The nurse who handled his triage could not get his blood. She tried multiple times and left him with a large bruise on his arm. Upset with her inabilities, I took both kids, and we went back for the taxi. We went back to the embassy and demanded that they find a pediatrician or another doctor to figure out what was wrong with Fred. Finally, we found a doctor who had graduated from Georgetown University. The moment we walked in and I described Fred's symptoms, the doctor took blood and x-rays. Immediately, he diagnosed Fred as having a softball-sized parasite in his stomach. Fred was restricted to liquids and Jell-O while his body got rid of the parasite. He ended up losing ten pounds.

After this ordeal, I realized that I needed to have confidence in my instincts and the choices I made for my family. I was parenting alone with a very sick child in a foreign country. The Colombia I knew was dangerous and potentially life-threatening every time we left home. I looked at each cab driver with suspicion, but I also knew that I would have to make difficult choices to ensure that Fred and Lori got the care that they deserved. If that meant that we would have to leave our secure confines to find a good doctor, so be it. I quickly realized that my role as an army wife was changing, and I was now responsible for making smart decisions for myself and the kids. Although these were tough, sobering realizations at first, I know these experiences helped me to become a strong, independent wife and mother in the coming years.

These tough times in Colombia—from the moment our plane flew out of Miami until we left this country—strengthened me and prepared me for many later trials in which I was required to roll with the punches. Things were going to be thrown at me for many years to come. I quickly learned that I would have to make moves alone and establish some semblance of normalcy while creating a home for the kids when my husband was overseas and not around to help us. In Colombia, I learned that it wasn't enough to merely appear to have things together. It was imperative that our lives be completely in order so that my children would not be affected by what was happening in their surroundings.

We survived the year only to learn that Freddie was going overseas again. This time, he would be stationed on the DMZ in Korea, and his tour would be unaccompanied. The kids and I moved back to San Antonio where I could be close to home. We bought a house, and because Freddie left immediately, I was left with the power of attorney to sign everything and get us situated in our brand new home. I was responsible for the landscaping and decorating the interior. My father helped me put in the grass and flowerbed, and my mom was a tremendous help, too. Because Freddie and I maintained two households, I worked to help supplement our income. I never wanted the kids to come home to an empty house, but with two households, I was forced to do just that.

The year went by quickly, and before we knew it, we were off again. This time it was to Maryland where Freddie worked at NSA. We lived in Columbia, Maryland. Living on the East Coast was a totally different experience for us. There was a different attitude generally, lots more traffic, and four distinct seasons. We were there for six months when Freddie learned that he was being sent on another mission. General Merritt called him for a secret assignment, and I didn't learn until later that he was working in El Salvador.

Once again, I was alone. This was the second year of the next three years that the kids and I would be on our own. I worked as a merchandiser at a large department store to make ends meet, and this time I was lucky enough to be able to negotiate my own hours. I went to work an hour before the store opened so that I was home when the kids arrived home from school.

At the same time, I lived through what would be the most tragic year of my life. In 1984, my parents came to visit us in Maryland. My mom came home with us after Christmas, and my father joined her a month later. The day before they were scheduled to leave, my dad suffered a massive stroke while visiting a friend in Rockville, Maryland. This was a stressful time, as the kids were in school, and I had to drive to the hospital an hour away in the winter weather to see my dad. Additionally, because all of my siblings lived in Texas, it was up to me to make some difficult decisions with little guidance from the rest of them. After two months of hospital care, the doctors gave him a pacemaker and stabilized him enough to transport him back to San Antonio.

In May, one of Freddie's uncles died suddenly. Then in September, Freddie's only paternal male cousin was beaten to death. On Freddie Junior's birthday, November 27, my mother complained of chest pains. Four days later, when she was finally taken to the hospital, we learned that she had suffered a massive heart attack. On December 15, my mother's youngest brother died and five days later my mother would follow. We buried her on December 22. Even though I had spent every moment of her last twenty days with her, it was the worst Christmas holiday of my life. After dealing with the tragedy of her death, I left my family and went back to Maryland to mourn alone.

During that time, Freddie was assigned to the Armed Forces Staff College in Virginia. He had been given time off to attend the funeral but was forced to return shortly thereafter. It was incredibly difficult for me to force myself to get out of bed and function normally every day, but I knew I had to do it not only for myself but for my children. The sadness of my loss was overwhelming, but I could not let the weight of it consume me. Now that Freddie was gone again, I was the only adult in our household, and it was up to me to keep our home functioning.

Shortly thereafter, Freddie was relocated from Armed Forces Staff College in Virginia to Fort Sill, Oklahoma. Since the kids were in the middle of a school year, I decided it was best not to move them, and we stayed by ourselves on the East Coast for the duration of the school year. Finally, in the summer of 1985, we moved to Lawton, Oklahoma. Since the kids were older, I was able to spend more time volunteering. During those three years, I became a volunteer for hospice and a rape crisis center. These were the most rewarding paid or unpaid jobs I ever had. There were times that I would spend the entire day with a terminal patient. There were other times when I was notified by pager in the middle of the night that a woman had been raped, and I was needed down at the hospital to comfort her. It was both rewarding and therapeutic to work with the ill and with victims. I missed my mother terribly, but my focus on helping others cope during difficult times made life more meaningful.

Again, Freddie was "highly selected" to command a battalion in Augsburg, Germany. Luckily, we were assigned to the First of the Thirty-sixth Field Artillery in beautiful southern Germany. We made the transition during the middle of the school year. Lori was a junior, and Fred was in eighth grade. They were at the age where they had made good friends, and both had become very involved with athletics. Needless to say, they were not happy to be plucked out of their school and forced to move in the middle of a school year to frigid Germany in the dead of winter. To make matters more frustrating, after we had packed up and prepared for our move, we waited in San Antonio for Freddie, who was again involved with a special overseas mission. After a month, we arrived in Germany. For the first thirty days, we stayed in a hotel, and then they moved us to temporary quarters. Just when we unloaded our household goods, we were told that we were moving into our permanent quarters.

Despite the initial struggles, the kids quickly acclimated to their new home. All the years of trying to instill confidence in them and teaching them that they can and will survive difficult times paid off. They immediately made soccer teams, and the next year they each ran for class president and won.

Freddie's change of command was July 11, 1988, and the following week he was sent to Grafenwohr for three weeks. The second day after arrival, a soldier tragically lost his life. I was, therefore, immediately faced with assisting a wife that I had never met and who had just found out earlier that day that she was pregnant. Although there was tragedy at the onset of the command, this ended up being one of our better assignments. The kids excelled. Lori was the captain of her varsity soccer team, the All-European female golfer, the senior class president, and she was accepted into the University of Texas. Fred played for the junior varsity soccer team, was ranked fourth in his age group as a golfer throughout the Department of Defense Education Agency, and became his freshman class president.

During my time in Germany, God put a very special person in my life: Inge Kick, who was in the German-American club. We met at one of their luncheons, became fast friends and have remained close ever since. She has come to see me in a number of our duty stations and I, in turn, have returned to lovely Augsburg to see her and her family.

I guess there are no words to describe the pain and agony of a child leaving home, especially when the child leaves to go to school on the other side of the ocean thousands of miles away. In 1989, Lori graduated from high school and left Augsburg to attend the University of Texas. Luckily, the next four months went by quickly, and she was able to return home for Christmas. During the time when she first left, the dynamics of our household changed. Although I knew she missed us terribly, the three of us were having a difficult time making the transition, as well.

When she returned for the spring semester, I felt that loss once again, but this time there were other changes going on as well. The health of my father deteriorated, so I returned home to Texas to see him and be with my siblings. I spent thirty days with my father at the Veteran's Administration (VA) Hospital while he was in a coma. On the day I flew home to Germany accompanied by Lori, who was starting her summer vacation, we received the call that my father had passed away. The Red Cross assisted the four of us in returning to San Antonio.

The three years in Germany went by quickly. Freddie was gone a lot of the time, preparing his soldiers for the Gulf War. He worked to prepare them for their own fight, while I prepared their families for the inherent struggles that arise when a family is left alone overseas and their soldier is fighting in a war. Being in the United States and knowing the language makes life so much easier. But I was proud of the women I helped, because they remained in Germany while the battalion fought in the Gulf War. Unfortunately, Freddie got a different assignment to the Inter-American Defense College (IADC) in Washington, D.C., during the war. He wasn't able to see firsthand the impressive results of the work and time that he had given to his battalion. We all knew, though, that his soldiers were well-trained and prepared for anything that came their way. In addition, I knew that the families who remained in Germany were equally prepared to hold down the fort while their soldiers were away.

Within six months of living in Virginia, Freddie was called for another special mission. Seven months later I found out that Fred and I would be leaving our home in Fairfax and going on to Lima, Peru.

Once again, Fred was plucked from his school and his friends, and he was to spend his senior year in another foreign country. By this time, we were both accustomed to making ourselves comfortable in a foreign country. However, Lima was afflicted by civil unrest, inflation was rampant, and the city was ravished by poverty and a cholera epidemic. The beleaguered government was struggling with two insurgent warring factions: Sendero Luminoso, better known as Shining Path, and the MRTA. Bombings were frequent occurrences in the city, and our house became a fortress. Metal bars deterred trespassers looking to enter our front courtyard, and ten-foot walls with shards of glass at the top surrounded the backyard. We kept guns in every room in case we were faced with an intruder.

I worked at the APO at the American Embassy, so Freddie and I were able to travel together to and from work. Every day was an adventure. We took different routes to work to ensure that no one was following us and to be sure that we never dropped our guard. Even though these were dangerous conditions, we had a wonderful time in Lima and made a number of good friends who were also stationed at the embassy. Since Lima was under a curfew, everyone had to be in by nine o'clock in the evening. Obviously, Fred Junior's social calendar was quite limited. Despite that, he made wonderful friends and excelled in high school.

The day we arrived in Lima, I was told that I would be the Chairwoman for the ambassador's Christmas party. Ambassador Tony and Susan Quainton had consistently given an annual party for approximately four hundred special needs children who lived in the surrounding areas of town. Planning the party was a snap; at this point in my army career, I had planned and hosted a number of high volume functions. But in this case, there were the challenges of entering dangerous locations when we dropped off the invitations, going into the local community to obtain necessary items, and soliciting large, local businesses for money.

Luckily, we survived Fred Junior's last year in high school. It was very difficult for me to let go of my baby, but I was relieved when he decided to return to San Antonio to attend St. Mary's University. Our extended family was still in San Antonio, and Lori was only an hour away, finishing up her senior year at the University of Texas. I was thrilled that I would not have to worry about bombings or waiting every second for Fred's return whenever he left.

From Lima we departed for a totally different assignment. We were stationed in Fort Drum, New York, approximately twenty miles from the Canadian border. For two Texas natives, the winter in Fort Drum was the most challenging we had ever faced. There were times when we watched the news, and the national forecast would dub Watertown, New York—the city where Fort Drum was located—the coldest city in the United States. There were times when the temperature was forty degrees below with the wind chill factor. The winter forecast was snow, snow, and more snow, so I became the snow-blowing queen. Thank goodness for the good friends that lived around us, including Colonel Kip and Joyce Ward, Colonel Jim and Carol Campbell, Colonel Evan and Benita Gaddis, Colonel Andy and Nicky Berdy, Colonel Jim Dubik, Colonel Mike and Barbara Dallas, and Brigadier General Greg and Glennace Gile.

Freddie was a Division Artillery, or Divarty, commander so I again was faced with helping other wives. While in command, he was deployed to Somalia, and upon his return, his unit was then sent to Haiti. Lori was anxiously awaiting her acceptance to law school and moved in with me during the Haiti deployment.

My biggest accomplishment was establishing a food pantry at Fort Drum. It allowed not only the Divarty family members but any and all soldiers stationed at Fort Drum to benefit from the pantry's resources. Even though our division commander did not believe that there would be a need for this food pantry, I continued to make it happen. He was genuinely surprised to learn later on that I had eighty-seven soldiers with over four hundred dependents using the facility throughout the year.

I have very little complaints about the various duty stations we lived at, although there were obviously some I preferred over others. Panama turned out to be the crown jewel of all of our tours. We had the comfort of knowing that our children were together. Lori decided to attend law school at St. Mary's School of Law where Fred was completing his last year of undergraduate studies. They opted to be roommates, which was a tremendous comfort for us.

Freddie and I were surrounded by beautiful scenery, and our house was on Fort Amador, Panama. About fifteen yards from our front door, we looked out onto the third hole of the Amador Golf Course and the Atlantic Ocean on the horizon. I was fortunate enough to have a lovely home and be a part of the history of Panama. In the early 1900s, the French started the Panama Canal but left in 1903 because of the yellow fever epidemic. The Americans came in to complete the task of the Panama Canal project. Because the Americans did not officially turn over Amador until December 31, 1999, we were the last couple to live in this historical house at Fort Amador.

Again we were blessed with wonderful friends. We enjoyed many rounds of golf and lots of partying with good friends like Colonel Larry and Sharon Gregg, Lieutenant Colonel Bill and Ellie Anderson, Chief Warrant Officer 3 Paul and Laura McDill, and Department of the Army Civilians (DAC) Richard and Angie Linton. Perhaps one of the best relationships we had in our military career was with our USARSO (U.S. Army South) Commander General Lawson MacGruder and his wife, Gloria.

We moved to Fort Clayton on the Pacific side of the Panama Canal and awaited our next assignment. Freddie was selected for brigadier general, and we were excited to be able to celebrate with the great friends that we had made while living in Panama. They were as happy for us and as proud of us as we were for ourselves.

As usual, after another year we were off again. We went to Fort Stewart, Georgia, but we were assigned to Hunter Army Airfield in Savannah, one of the most beautiful, historical areas in Georgia. Freddie became the assistant division commander of support (ADCS). We were involved with our church and the civilian community. So involved were we, in fact, that Freddie was named grand marshal for the annual St. Patrick's Day parade. Of course, I just couldn't help but chuckle at the request—once again, his tiny bit of Irish blood from many generations back came through. The laugh was on me when I realized the enormity of the parade. It is one of the biggest in the country and is comparable to the St. Patrick's Day parades in Boston and New York.

About two weeks after the parade, Freddie injured his back and was told to lay low for the next few months until he was ready to deploy to Kuwait. In December, before his deployment, he had back surgery. Once up and around, he was able to travel, and he left with the division to Kuwait. Two weeks after he was gone, I had arthroscopic surgery on my back. Right after returning home from the hospital, I received a phone call from a Charlie Wilhelm who explained to me matter-of-factly that he was the SOUTH-Com commander. I didn't understand the magnitude of the phone call or the significance of this commander's role. General Wilhelm was a four-star general and was calling to interview Freddie for the deputy commander in chief position (DCINC) of SOUTHCom. I explained to the general that Freddie was in Kuwait, but as soon as I was able to make contact with him, I would extend the message to him.

When Freddie called and heard about the message, he thought it was for one of the joint operations or strategy and policy positions. I explained that the general wanted to interview him for the DCINC position. When Freddie called the general, he found out that he was being considered for this position because he was on the two-star general list. Freddie was eventually chosen and served under General Wilhelm as the DCINC for two years as a frocked two-star general in Miami, Florida.

Before Freddie started his new position in June 1998, Lori graduated from law school, and later that year she was licensed to practice law in Texas. Our family was very proud of her. Lori graduated on the same day that Freddie interviewed with General Wilhelm; Freddie flew from Kuwait, went to his interview and arrived in time to see Lori cross the stage at her graduation ceremony.

We quickly learned that we had been blessed to work with the Wilhelms, certainly one of the most outstanding military couples we ever encountered in our joint career. They were knowledgeable, they were visionaries, and they exhibited compassion and sincerity in all of their actions. Valerie was the epitome of the Southern belle, exuding Southern charm, grace, and hospitality while wooing the ladies from Central and South America. What a couple they were!

While in Florida, rather than living on base, we lived in the civilian community and were still able to make a number of both civilian and military friends. In fact, I brought several neighbors together who had lived in that neighborhood for years but had never known each other, much less the military families. My neighbors met and mingled for the first time, and we eventually formed a dinner club. One neighbor would choose a restaurant, and we would all enjoy the venue together.

The military friends I had in Miami also enjoyed a breakfast group. The group consisted of Maria Elena Sanchez, Gail Goodman, and Valerie Wilhelm. We would often spend the whole morning laughing until we finally got down to business. One matter of business was organizing a zip code coffee for each area. Our goal was to have each zip code have their own coffees so that everyone could receive information on all activities in the civilian sector and the military arena. Again, this was a wonderful assignment.

U.S. Army South, after being in Panama for one hundred years, was strategically moved to Puerto Rico to further deployments. After the two years in Miami, Freddie was given the command of USARSO. We arrived at the beautiful island of Puerto Rico in July 2000. During the two and a half years of Freddie's command, I was given the opportunity to accompany him on a number of his trips. I was fortunate to see and experience the wonderful people and diverse cultures throughout the Caribbean, Central America, and South America. On numerous occasions I was able to transport boxes of necessities and clothing to orphanages in the various countries. These trips became that much more special when I experienced true gratitude from the less fortunate whom we had served.

Despite the lovely scenery and the special opportunities that I enjoyed while we lived in Puerto Rico, it also turned out to be one of the most emotionally draining duty stations we ever had. All of the good times were overshadowed by the sadness that eventually took over our daily lives toward the end of our assignment. The turmoil began when the decision was made to move USARSO from Puerto Rico to San Antonio. Although Freddie was instrumental in securing a move for the unit to a different location, the move was done without personal motivation. As a result of the planned move, Freddie was attacked in the *The San Juan Star* newspaper, and there were many threats that eventually required security, and my safety was jeopardized. I suddenly became "the general's wife," but instead of it being said with pride and honor, it was said with disdain.

Although there is nothing that can be compared to the backlash we received from the island of Puerto Rico, our stay there would not have been tolerable but for the friendships we made, both in the military and in the civilian community. To this day, we frequently return to Puerto Rico to visit those friends. Those relationships helped us endure the stress that we encountered. Some of those friends include the Bicardi, Esteve, Rodriquez, and Fernandez families.

When the move to Fort Sam Houston occurred in 2003, it could not have come faster and at a better time. Emotionally, Puerto Rico had taken its toll. Luckily for the command, USARSO moved to Texas without any flaws. We had brought the command to a better location, and the soldiers were now on a stateside base. Personally, I could not have been happier. Fred had recently moved to San Antonio from Chicago, and Lori was practicing law as an assistant district attorney in San Antonio, so both of my children were again in the same city with me. Additionally, my extended family was still in San Antonio, and they eagerly welcomed us back into our family network.

Once we received orders as to where we would live, I could not have been happier. Our house on 11 Staff Row was a historical home. The house had previous occupants such as the famous William Travis from the Alamo to many commanding generals over the past one hundred years. Finishing our career in this lovely mansion and being stationed at the beautiful "Fort Sam" was a wonderful way to say goodbye to the army.

Of course, finishing our career at Fort Sam Houston was bittersweet. I would be remiss if I did not mention the friends that completed the last few years with us. Some of them I had made over the years, and others I became particularly close to during the difficult times in Puerto Rico. One such friend is Wendy Ruiz. Wendy is an Ecuadorian whose heart and soul belongs to her adopted country—the United States. She was my rock, my advisor, and my confidante. Wendy made bleak moments tolerable and all things possible.

We lived at Fort Sam Houston before turning over command and retiring. We would make the decision to leave the army in 2004. It was a difficult decision to make, because we weren't entirely sure what we wanted out of our future. On one hand, Freddie and I did not know anything different than the military way. For thirty-three years, we had lived a life that was surrounded by the comforts of the army and our military family.

However, returning home and renewing our relationship with our children helped us decide that we wanted to stay home. Lori had given us our first grandchild, and we also recognized, after the death of Freddie's sister, that our extended family was growing older. Both of these events helped solidify what we already knew in our hearts: we were ready to leave the military. We found a house in San Antonio and purchased it. We began to prepare ourselves for the world outside the barracks. On May 1, 2004, we hung up our combat boots and entered the civilian world.

Since 2004, a lot has happened in our lives. Just as we suspected, at times the transition has been difficult. I would venture to guess that Freddie has struggled more with the transition than I have. After all, I didn't lose the comforts of a daily job, an aide, and leaving a profession that I loved. For me, I was able to quickly acclimate to seeing my children and extended family and becoming a full-time grandmother. It is perhaps the greatest gift I have been given. I have found my calling, and I know that this is where we were meant to be. My grandchildren frequently remind me of the purpose for my existence here on earth.

Growing up, my mother would always tell us, "Lo que haces con tus padres, pagas con tus hijos," which translated means, "You will pay with your children, by how you treat your parents." I have found this statement to be completely true.

I have been blessed with two beautiful and outstanding young adults in my life. Both of my children are successful, and they reassure me daily in their demeanor and achievements that their childhood in the military did not hinder their ability to succeed in any way.

I can say that now I know I have done it all. I have lived the American dream. I have given many years to the military, and I am a better person and American for it. I have had the chance to see the world and meet a number of everlasting friends. I have also experienced the uniquely American challenge of being a Hispanic in a predominantly Caucasian institution. I have overcome overt racism and subtle discrimination, and many times, I was immersed in a culture in which I was the only minority.

I came from a close-knit Hispanic family who raised me to always put family first. Like many Latino women, I never expected to leave that security and move far away from home. Yet, I left my comfortable environment behind. While the adventures I enjoyed, and sometimes endured, with Freddie, Lori, and Fred Junior are priceless and unforgettable, I faced many cultural obstacles without being able to fall back on the loving hands of my parents. Typically, I was the only Hispanic officer's wife. Many times, I was forced to educate others about my background and dispel their misconceptions. I was faced with the naïveté of some who believed that all Hispanics are the same. When these people came to me with their preconceived notions about my heritage, education, and upbringing, I countered their ideas by highlighting my uniqueness and my devotion to my family, my husband's career, and our army's future success. In the end, I came to recognize that there really are no differences between us when it comes to defending our country and supporting those who put their lives on the line to protect the rest of us.

I therefore have my own challenge to give to the present and future wives of our proud soldiers: accept the beautiful differences that we have to offer, and instead of relying on labels to classify us as Hispanic Americans (Chicanos, Latinos, etc.), begin to recognize us as Americans who just happen to be Hispanic. Create a balance that steers away from racism and discrimination, and move toward a dynamic that embraces cultural differences, traditions, and heritage.

Now I am here and enjoying my family, all the while giving back to the community and hopefully acting as a mentor and role model for those military wives that will follow in my footsteps. As my husband continues his transition, I am reminded of the words of General Douglas MacArthur who said, "Old soldiers never die…they just fade away." By fading away, we have been able to renew our relationship and share in the gift of love for our grandchildren, our community, and the educational foundation that Freddie started here in San Antonio.

Up to this point, I have divulged the trials and tribulations of my military life as a spouse, a mother, and a role model. I now will attempt to put pen to paper to disclose the challenges I found that may help others learn to endure what was otherwise our lives in the military.

If a new military wife were to ask me for advice, I know that there are many things that I could offer. And yet, I would also have to point out the changes in the military over the past years. The biggest change is that many of the unique traditions, such as mandatory coffees that reflected on a husband's career, have become extinct. Wives used to be critical factors in their husband's promotions—we were even mentioned explicitly in officer efficiency reports. Military wives nowadays often have their own careers, and being a military spouse does not have the same meaning or role that it did when I was a young officer's wife. There isn't the level of participation and volunteering that we used to see fifteen to twenty years ago. Times have changed, and as a reflection of that, so has our army.

The most significant change occurred after the Gulf War. Before the war, there was no organized family support system. After the war, there was an interest in creating family support, and eventually it evolved to family readiness. Of course, those changes brought about new problems. Some wives literally took it as support when their husbands were gone. Rather than using it as a tool, they completely relied on the support group. Again, not the institution's fault, just a change of the times.

In the traditional career of an officer or an NCO, it was not uncommon for the family to move every year or two. Rarely did a family spend more than a couple of years in one place. In our careers we moved twenty-four times, but that is unheard of in today's army. The current family rarely has the same type of role as it used to. Our job as a family was to work toward Freddie's success as an officer. We each had a unique role to play. Our actions were always a reflection of him and his household. As part of the unit, the family had a responsibility to act appropriately, attend certain functions, and stay out of trouble.

Now that we have retired, I see that Freddie and I, as a married unit, have come full circle. We have come home and are reminded of the civilian life. This is not the same lifestyle for which we were groomed and for which we groomed others for thirty-three years. There isn't that sense of right and wrong, the sense of urgency, or a need to follow a protocol. Yet, we love being home. By getting involved in the community, we have tried to be examples not only to other young military personnel, but for all who want to go out into the world, explore, and find themselves.

Being a volunteer taught me how to be a better person. I learned how to give back to others in their time of need, even in my times of sorrow. I have a sincere affection for people who give their time generously. Because the military offered me the opportunity to give back, I know that I have given not only to others, but I have also given back to our country. My sacrifices as a wife allowed my family to make this country a better place to live.

By all appearances, it would appear that I should be bitter. I spent many years alone, raising two children without the assistance of a partner and maintaining a household with no other adult to rely on. But I harbor no grudges, and I would not change my life as a military wife. My parents taught me strength and gave me confidence, but it was the army that gave me my wings. Because I had to make it on my own, I am a stronger woman, and I have a very strong relationship with both of my children. I had the opportunity to give to others, and I have changed lives and learned from many of those whom I helped.

We are no longer General and Mrs. V; now we simply answer to Ya-Ya and Yo-Yo. What a treat that is for Freddie and me. Do we miss the army? Of course! But as Freddie buried the dead from the war, we have learned that life is short and it goes on. Just as the Bible says, it is the alpha, life's beginning, and the omega, life's end. We learned together that there is no greater love than that required to serve one's country and pay the ultimate sacrifice. We served our country proudly, and now, if we must give our lives, the institution has prepared us better than one can imagine.

I agree with Freddie that if the army had a better understanding of its soldiers and family, and if we better understood the army, our institution would be that much more formidable. This is our intent in telling our story: we want both parties to better understand each other. The army needs to do everything it can to understand the gift it has in its proud, Hispanic soldiers. But every Hispanic soldier needs to enter into service with open eyes and a willingness to serve and reach the highest level of achievement possible. Our new life is awesome, and we wouldn't trade it for anything. We hope that our input in these pages will better prepare soldiers and families for our nation's future challenges.

CHAPTER 7

MILITARY BRATS: THE CHALLENGE TOWARD OUR SUCCESS

Being a soldier's child is not just a mind-set; it is ingrained inside of me and makes up the fabric of my life. It molded my thoughts, goals, and attitudes that I will carry with me throughout my lifetime.
—Lori Valenzuela-McCleskey

It should be clear by now that my success in the army was a direct result of the support that my wife Esther provided day in and day out in our military career. My children Lori and Freddie were just as instrumental in the trajectory of my career. Although the usual expectation is that the parents support the kids, Esther and I both found that the children were just as capable of supporting us when we needed it. We instilled the idea early in them that whether we succeeded or failed, we would do it together. As a result, they were willing early on to take their share of the load in our family's endeavors.

Because of my career, I was never able to give my children a normal childhood with the stability that most children enjoy growing up. I could never guarantee them that they would be able to stay at the school they loved indefinitely. Nor could I promise them that their personal activities would always take precedence over the duties that the army imposed on me. In some ways, I feel like I overburdened them and, at times, misplaced my priorities, losing them in the mix. However, they never failed to amaze me with their resilience and willingness to be part of the team. They understood—as children almost always do—that the long-term success of our family was worth their sacrifices. Their experiences as military brats gave them a sense of selflessness and maturity beyond their years. I am proud of the people they were then and the people they have become. This is their story, in their words...

Lori

The first thing I remember after my first few days at the University of Texas at Austin (UT) was that the section of my dorm was segregated from the rest of the dormitory. Not physically segregated, just "color" segregated. I began my studies there in 1989, so this arrangement may seem almost impossible; however, anyone who attended school there at that time knows that there were periods of racial unrest. My parents were stationed in Augsburg, Germany. My younger brother Freddie was beginning his sophomore year in high school. I had never lived in Austin, but I left my family behind to come to the United States and embark on the most challenging time in my life.

In 1989, the University of Texas was a small city with a population of fifty thousand students. Leaving a high school graduating class of approximately eighty-five people, the size of the university came as quite a shock. I decided to live in one of the smallest all-female dorms, which had three floors with three hallways on each floor and was shaped like an H. Not understanding Texas weather, as I had only spent short periods of time in Texas, I didn't realize that when I signed up for the non-air-conditioned dorm, I was signing up for hell—or a place equally as warm.

My family dropped me off that first day, and we began unpacking my belongings. Within hours, I met my college roommate. She was a tiny African American from Dallas named Rhonda. We connected immediately, and despite my initial reservations about being so far away from home, I was confident that the school year to follow would prove to be one of the most exciting times in my life. Rhonda and I met our hallmates in the hours and days that followed our own introduction. Unlike the rest of the dorm, we quickly noticed that our hallway consisted only of Hispanics and African Americans. Basically, each room consisted of two females, one from each race. Further investigation proved that we, in fact, were the only hall that had any minorities. With the exception of one room that housed two black women, one of whom was a Longhorn cheerleader, we appeared to be a token group. We tagged ourselves members of the "minority hall" and attempted to make ourselves elite, not unique. We even went so far as to make a banner for our hallway. Upon questioning our resident assistant, we were told that we were placed in this setup so that we would have an easier time acclimating to our new environment.

At eighteen years old, the thought that I needed to be surrounded by people of my own race was shocking. In fact, this experience is one that I have carried with me, not because I felt scarred or oppressed in any way, but simply because I could not understand why someone would believe that I would feel more comfortable in this type of environment. I had spent my entire life around various ethnic groups and races and didn't feel the need at this time in my life to start being paired with other minorities to fit in and feel comfortable. Suddenly I was forced to accept that I was different—noticeably different—and I realized that I had left my colorblind environment the day I became student at the University of Texas.

Before UT, I had spent my entire life as an army brat. My parents spent thirty-three years in the military, and even though they retired three years ago, being a brat still permeates my life choices every day. Most people would assume that being a brat ends when she leaves home or perhaps when her parents retire; for a small percentage, that may be true. But most of us are brats forever. In fact, I remain true to my military roots and upbringing. Being a soldier's child is not just a mind-set; it is ingrained inside of me and makes up the fabric of my life. It molded my thoughts, goals, and attitudes that I will carry with me throughout my lifetime. Due to some of the struggles that I overcame as a military child, I am a stronger woman now than I would have been otherwise. My rearing in a military environment is part of who I am as a daughter, wife, mother, sister, and professional, and it infiltrates every emotion and attitude that accompanies those roles.

I am able to draw from my background the values and education that come from growing up as an army brat. Not only as a brat, but also as a child growing up in the house of a Hispanic soldier. Some of these lessons I have learned in hindsight, and others come filtering into my life when I express an opinion about my political posture, our military, the government, and the importance of family. When I say something or have a particular thought, I am aware of how the military molded my life—how the experiences, both good and bad, made me the person I am today.

The first lesson takes me back to my UT dorm experience. Perhaps one of the most endearing qualities of living the military lifestyle is that I don't remember noticing race when I was growing up. Although it may seem naïve or even silly, race was a nonissue to me. I went to nine different schools from kindergarten through high school. Many of our moves were during the summer, so almost every school year, I had to start all over and make new friends. It did not matter what race or ethnicity a person was—that first person who invited me to lunch, defended me, or asked me if I was new became my ally immediately. They could have been brown, white, black, or green for that matter, and I would not have cared. To have that initial acceptance was such a warm feeling for me as the new kid on the block. It wasn't that I was unaware of color or physical attributes, it was that it didn't matter to me. As such, I was always relieved to meet people who were drawn to me based on my interests alone whenever I entered a new environment.

Over the years, many of my enduring friendships were with other military brats. Frequently, those friendships began quickly and grew strong early in the relationship. Knowing that a person is a brat catapults us past that initial small talk and directly to more important matters. I already grasp their background and immediately empathize, because I have been there, too. I already know that they left their extended family and have moved repeatedly. They, too, have started over multiple times and have played for various athletic organizations. They are familiar with the difficulty of leaving one school curriculum and going to another that may be way ahead or far behind the previous one. Military brats already have all of that in common with a mere introduction, regardless of gender or race.

In hindsight, I recognize that we were the only Hispanic officer's family in almost every place we lived. We looked different, ate different food, and enjoyed special holidays and traditions. In fact, my parents in a very subtle way acknowledged that we were ethnically unique, but not in a way that made us feel separated or unusual. If someone had asked me then, I could tell him that I knew my friends came from completely different backgrounds, but once we left the confines of our individual homes, we were all part of one big family—the military family.

One division I do remember was officers' children versus enlisted children. I do not remember it as an issue of superiority or inferiority, but I recall that there was a separation—a physical separation—that existed when we lived on military bases. Living on a military base typically means living around those of a similar rank. In other words, higher field grade officers lived near and around other high grade field officers. Likewise, an enlisted family lived near other enlisted families. I cannot be certain, but my suspicion is that officers' children hung out with officers' children more, and enlisted children played with enlisted children more because of proximity rather than actual discrimination. Like many other groupings in the military, there is a preexisting separation when one is an officer versus an enlisted soldier. By default, I believe it filters down to the children.

The second life lesson that I learned is that a military family has to stick together. The bond of a military family is one that is unprecedented, because when we move to different cities, there is no one else but our family. Sometimes we went weeks without meeting any friends after a relocation. In times like these, a sibling and a parent are one's only friends. They become confidantes, pals, and they are a shoulder to cry on. A brother may play dolls with his sister in the same way his sister will play baseball with him without question.

The camaraderie built within a family unit is a bond that goes on for many years beyond the moment when a brat moves from her parents' home. When a brat leaves home to work or attend college, she is leaving behind the unit that moved with her, cried with her, rejoiced with her, and experienced a way of life that extended family or her spouse will never really appreciate. Families see their soldier off on tours with no date of return. They have seen other countries and packed and unpacked their lives over and over again. They know the struggles that accompany the absence of a soldier and the disruption that ensues when he returns. They know that there are secrets only family will share and hardships that no one else could imagine.

The connection I continue to share with my immediate family is one that most people cannot understand. They remain my closest friends, and even though I have been living on my own and with my husband and children for almost eighteen years, I still enjoy seeing my parents and brother every day. Even when the distance was more than a few miles apart, I made a connection with my family every day, either by mail or by phone. Although difficult and certainly different than their own family experiences, my husband and my sister-in-law have learned that we still have a strong tie to our parents. We still defer to them and trust their perspectives when making even the most mundane decisions. As a family, we spend vacations together and enjoy most of our weekends together. In fact, my mom remains my closest friend and confidante.

I have learned as an adult, and particularly as a mother, the unique and important roles that parents play in a military family. I now value the magnificent role that my mother played not only as a wife, but also as a military spouse. As is the case with the majority of military families, my father was the soldier, and my mom was everything else. She was the cook, the mechanic, the disciplinarian, the guardian, the hostess, and everything in between. Mom was responsible for herself, my brother and I regardless of whether she was sad, tired, or having a bad day.

Mom lost both of her parents during our travels and still had to come "home," away from her family, to continue to raise her military family. Despite that heartache, she found time to volunteer, work with other military spouses, host gatherings at our house, and make sure that our household functioned on a daily basis. She insisted that our family remain an intact unit. We waited to have dinner together every night and tried to spend time daily with each other as a family. She helped us cope through transitions and found a way to make every duty station feel like home.

Mom taught us that having the right attitude is of the utmost importance. Being a military wife, she showed love of family, love of army, and love of nation. She remains one of the most patriotic women I know and helped mold our patriotic roots. Her sense of dedication to our nation still permeates her life. The importance of loving ourselves and loving our extended family came from her guidance. She helped us to find ourselves spiritually and to know that there is a higher being. She continues to be a daily reminder that times can be tough, and the only solution is to learn to cope and move forward. Despite all of the personal difficulties she faced, she kept moving and always maintained a positive perspective.

When I am home alone with my children for extended periods of time, I remember when she was alone for up to a year at a time. Days when my husband works late or is gone overnight, I recall the many moves that my mom made alone and the time when she slept alone, not knowing when or if my father would return. When I am in an unfamiliar environment, I look to her example for strength. She was stationed in new city after new city with no friends, no family, and little knowledge about the military life. When we were new to a location, she was also new. Somehow, she would acclimate quickly and never let on that there were times she was as frightened and lonely as we were. She taught me the importance of emotional strength, the willingness to give of myself to others, to be a role model, to have a strong faith, and to know that as a woman there is nothing I cannot conquer. Above all, she is my example of how to be a good mother.

As a parent and a professional, I understand the hardships my father endured. Despite the fact that my mother worked several years, my father was the primary breadwinner. He was responsible for making sure we were taken care of while trying to fight his own wars—quite literally. It takes a special kind of hero—like my dad—to leave his loved ones behind, knowing that he may never return. Aside from his personal endeavors, he had the awesome responsibility of commanding young soldiers into combat all the while trying to be a role model for other Hispanics.

What I didn't realize all of those years of watching my dad get into uniform, leave early, stay late, pack up, and go to foreign nations for months on end is that he loved the service. He loved his commitment to the military and loved knowing that even if he only affected one soldier's life, Hispanic or not, that he had done his job. If he brought back soldiers from a combat zone with the entire unit intact and with no lives lost, he fulfilled his promise to their families. He remained passionate and faithful to his love of the army until his last day of service. That passion resonates in my life and my career choices. I can appreciate that love for a profession and the importance of caring for others and serving as a positive example. His service to our nation—without much pay or glamour—is something I admire about him. He is the person I can thank for my interest in my government position, a position that often requires long hours with little monetary reward but serves for me as a pillar of my being. He has shown me how to succeed while maintaining happiness and self worth, the importance of education, and above all, that there will be other Hispanics who will look to my example. For that reason, I have strived to be the best that I can be.

I cannot pinpoint which parent taught me about giving to others, whether it was by way of material items, monetary donations, or time, but I learned early on that we were all placed on this earth to assist others in any way possible. I remember growing up and being forced to learn that many are less fortunate than us. When someone didn't have a place to eat a meal, they came to our dinner table, and when someone needed a place to stay, they were welcome in our home. My parents both taught me that there are always places to volunteer or opportunities to extend to others a helping hand.

Aside from showing us the importance of helping others, my parents also did a great job in teaching us to be colorblind in terms of race but to maintain pride in our ethnicity and our heritage. They made a point to bring us back to our hometown of San Antonio at least a few times a year so that we could appreciate our family and culture. They believed in the strength of family and thought we should have a relationship with our first cousins and our grandparents. They understood that traditions are not learned but taught through experiences and family history. Now, my family, my brother and his wife, and my parents have all settled in San Antonio. We came back "home."

As a military child, I learned the cardinal rule: home is where your parents are stationed. Relocating in the middle of a school year to move to a different country is difficult, but somehow the new duty station became our new home. We learned early on that celebrating Christmas or Easter can be done in any city and in any country and that home is always where are parents are located.

As an officer's child, I was educated in the importance of following rules. A parent in a commanding position educates others on regulations and reprimands when there is a lack of compliance. There is an ongoing sense of responsibility and pressure to do the right thing. This is particularly true when living on a base. I learned the rules early on about the respect of rank and proper etiquette.

There are things called "blotters" that allow everyone on the base to know any kind of trouble or problems that the military police may have had. A parent's boss sees this and knows if a soldier's children have gotten into trouble. Our behavior spoke directly to the way we were being raised and to the kind of job our father was doing "commanding" his household.

The importance of doing the "right thing" has followed me into my current role as a prosecutor. I know what is right and what is wrong, and I appreciate the importance of integrity. There are fundamental rules that apply to everyone, and my line of work allows me to punish those who fail to live up to that standard. The importance of laws and rules comes from my upbringing and my life in the military. I was told early on that my word was my bond, and I was expected to follow through on my commitments.

I became knowledgeable early on about the importance of acclimating to any situation, and it is a rare day that I find myself uncomfortable in any environment. I frequently stand in front of a jury with little hesitation or fear that I will not find my way into a comfort zone, despite never having met my panel. I attend parties and know that I will quickly meet others and find common interests for the sake of conversation, if only for a few minutes. After all, treading into unknown territory with unfamiliar faces is the way I spent the first half of my life.

Despite my ability to easily find my comfort zone as an adult, I don't miss the gypsy lifestyle from my youth. Every once in a while, I will tell my husband I would like to move, but I think I feel this way because I miss suitcases, moving into a new place where I can start over, and rearranging my furniture. Truthfully, I would probably be fine if we never moved and if I could raise my children with the same friends for the next eighteen years. At times, I miss my nomadic childhood, but now I find that roots and a home in one city are not so horrible.

When I think of military friends with whom I still keep in contact, I realize that there are some common threads. Many of us joined the military, work for government positions, or married someone in one of those fields. Many of us have succeeded in our careers, and few of us have gotten into legal trouble. Many of us started families of our own and are adopting the standards and values that our parents instilled in us. We are confidant, accomplished, and we know where we came from. As adults, we meet other brats and immediately relate. Our bonds pass the test of time, and we can instantly reconnect after going for years without talking.

Military brats are taught early on to love their country. I love this nation and all of the freedoms that we enjoy. Because of my upbringing, my heart lurches and a smile spreads across my face when I see or hear something patriotic. A twenty-one-gun salute or "Taps" brings tears to my eyes, even when I see it in a movie. My heart aches for the family member who receives the flag folded in that perfect triangle at a military funeral. I love the National Anthem and think the stars and stripes flying in the wind against a blue sky is one of the most beautiful sights that any American can witness. I watch the news each night with dread that we have lost another soldier in war—a son, a sister, a father. I see soldiers in uniform and smile at them. Our shared smile is one of understanding.

I know that there are people fighting for us every day to keep the nation that we enjoy—I know because I lived with one for years. I have the utmost respect when a wounded soldier who has lost a limb or will never walk again says that she would go back tomorrow if she could, because she wants to return and fight alongside her military family. The bond that is created by the soldiers with their comrades in arms and the institution is amazing to me, and it's something that most civilians cannot truly understand. In fact, I often wonder why we as a nation have not implemented some type of mandatory military service so that everyone can appreciate the service and sacrifice of our soldiers. Despite my occasional frustrations with politicians and the action or inaction of our government, I still believe that we live in the best country in the world.

Now that I am a parent and back in my parents' hometown, I recognize how far our Hispanic family went in the military. My parents did not have much growing up. Neither one of them had lived in another city—much less another country—before my father was commissioned. My mother's parents didn't even finish high school. My father became a general at a time when Hispanic generals were not the norm. He spent five years as the highest-ranking active duty Hispanic general.

I look back and see the trials that my parents faced. They did not grow up in military families, yet they persevered and made it to the top. Our hometown knows that our family is one that succeeded despite the odds. This city did not forget that they sent off two young adults who returned as two accomplished military leaders and who proved themselves throughout their many years of achievement.

I must also discuss, though, the negative aspects of growing up in a military family. It is difficult to not attend school reunions or have friends that I went to school with from kindergarten to high school just down the street. I will never know what it is like to grow up with the same group of friends and to live in the same house or neighborhood my whole life. Because many of us came from different parts of the world, we left Europe and scattered all over the United States and abroad. Just finding everyone from my high school graduation would prove a daunting task, much less trying to find others who attended the eight other schools I attended.

Unfortunately, the army is not always a grateful institution. It does not appreciate the difficulty in living in certain parts of the world and moving in the middle of a school year. It does not always recognize those soldiers that should be recognized. When a soldier does not follow the right path or does something that tarnishes the army's reputation, the army will hang that soldier out, despite his or her years of faithful service. At times, the army does not remember that there is a family behind each soldier that has given up their own opportunities and careers to follow its soldier.

What is perhaps the biggest struggle as a military brat is the realization that with his or her soldier's commitment to the army comes the hard fact that there will be times that the institution comes first. A soldier's marriage to the military may supersede his marriage to his family—not just some of the time, but the entire time the soldier is on active duty. I can look back and see that many of our wants and needs took a backseat to the army's needs. There were many times that we had to leave a school with a great curriculum or extracurricular activities. I remember playing sports for a city with various advanced leagues and going to a duty station the subsequent year that didn't even have an athletic program. A military family is a team, but all too often the team captain—the soldier—dictates what the other teammates will do and where they will go.

But overall, I was blessed to be a soldier's child. I was able to experience firsthand many things that others never get to in their lifetime. I was able to travel by plane, train, and boat to other countries. I learned Spanish by immersion in the culture in Colombia rather than from a textbook. I was able to see places only those with great wealth get to see. Because of the military, I saw many places in our country, Europe, and South America. I have seen the blue Mediterranean in Greece and the beauty of the view from the heights of Machu Picchu. As a graduating senior, I was able to go to the Austrian Alps, I played golf in Berlin before the wall came down, and I have driven on the German freeways with no speed limit. I can appreciate that I have electricity and that I do not have to worry daily if my neighborhood or my house will be blown up by guerillas. I don't worry that bombs will go off at night as I enjoy the leisure and comforts of my home.

If given the opportunity, I would not have changed my life as an army brat. My childhood, unique only to other military children, is a fortunate upbringing. For most of us, our memories of military life are fond ones. The experiences that we had continue to inform us in our day-to-day life. As a military child, I am proud of the heroics of my father, who fought with pride for our nation, and I am indebted to my mother, who stayed home and raised us.

I am proud of my culture, and in the rare instances when my race, gender, and political preferences are held against me, I handle it with the finesse and strength that comes from my upbringing. I am constantly reminded of my spirit, my passion, and the values I hold dearest. First and foremost, I am an army brat, and there is nothing more rewarding than being a soldier's child.

Freddie Junior

"Are you Major Valenzuela's son?"
"Are you Lieutenant Colonel Valenzuela's son?"
"Are you Colonel Valenzuela's son?"
"Are you General Valenzuela's son?"

Over the years, I can track my father's rise in rank through the army based on questions like these. Even being out on my own for at least fourteen years now, with a name like Alfred Valenzuela Jr., this question is still posed to me on a weekly, if not daily, basis. I am proud to say, "Yes, that is my father."

I followed in the footsteps of my father and grandfather, attending St. Mary's University in San Antonio, Texas. In my grandfather's time there, he and my grandmother were remarried in the St. Mary's gym, knowing that she was pregnant with my father. Who would have guessed that as an adult, he would not only attend classes there, but he would be an integral part of their rich ROTC program and later become a two-star general in the U.S. Army? I started to veer from my father's military path when I arrived in 1992 for my freshman year at St. Mary's. My brilliant father decided to call the ROTC department ahead of my arrival, just to make sure I'd follow a "straight and narrow" path. Although his intentions were good, it only made things worse for me. Needless to say, my stint in the St. Mary's ROTC lasted only one semester. Instead of forging a bond with other ROTC cadets, I became a part of another brotherhood in the Sigma Phi Epsilon fraternity.

My father has set an amazing example of perseverance, leadership, and love for family and country that resonates in my daily life. Though I didn't choose the military track for my own life, I apply many of the same principles in my own career.

Currently, I am a senior program manager with experience in multiple fields. I have worked for two public housing authorities, several construction companies, and I currently work in the educational testing industry. Because of my well-traveled upbringing, I operate comfortably in most situations. My interaction with people from different countries, backgrounds, and perspectives allows me to quickly adapt to my surroundings. In my professional and daily life, I can say that the most important values my parents and my military upbringing instilled in me are the importance of respect, courtesy, and hard work. I learned early on to always respect my elders and to treat strangers with the same courtesy I would show my family and friends. And I learned that if I wanted to advance in any field, I would have to put in long hours, and nothing would be given to me for free. I feel that these basic principles have contributed to who I am today.

Although my parents, my sister, and I may have physically moved numerous times during my childhood, I can't imagine a more stable family and home life. The support that we provided to each other was the backbone of our family.

My earliest memories are of Colombia, South America; I can remember my mother, my sister, and I arriving at the airport in Bogotá. We were a month delayed, due to the kidnapping of the U.S. ambassador to Colombia. My mother, the ever-diligent military wife, packed up and traveled countless miles with us, always ready to join her husband at his new duty assignment.

I know it was hard for my mother to be away from her parents and siblings in San Antonio, but we spoke with them every chance we had. For my grandparents' forty-second wedding anniversary, we surprised them by all flying in to celebrate. Mom and Dad packed me up in a TV box and wheeled me in before Momo and Popo Trevino. I jumped out of the box and gave them the biggest surprise they may have ever had. Poor Momo and Popo thought my crazy parents had shipped me all the way from Colombia with no food or water. Luckily, the joy of seeing my family overcame my grandparents' fear that their grandson had been mailed back to Texas in a box.

No matter where we lived, we still had wonderful moments like this that make us laugh to this day. We could show up for the holidays and pick up right where we left off. It never felt like we were alone. We knew we had each other, and we also had a huge family just waiting to see us whenever the chance arose.

Coming from such a large family, I never felt alone. No matter where we lived, we took our traditions and experiences with us. Whether I was eating warm, homemade tortillas at my grandma's house in San Antonio or dancing to Casey Kasem's Top Forty on the weekends with my mom and sister on the other side of the Atlantic, we were always at home. We always had a sense of self, and it allowed us to fit in everywhere.

It wasn't until I was a junior in high school, in Alexandria, Virginia, that I asked my mother, "What am I?" The military is a diverse environment to grow up in; as such, the color of my skin and the sound of my last name were never considered a topic for discussion. Race really did not become a prevalent issue until I entered college, where young adults struggle to define themselves and are perpetually required to fill out paperwork that classify them. I was raised to think of myself as an American first and a Hispanic second, and I proudly hold onto that philosophy to this day.

As a child, I was aware of my father's rank in the army and that he was successful, but his success as a *Hispanic* officer never occurred to me. I realized the importance of his ethnic background and how it related to his military experience when he was assigned to the Inter-American Defense College, where he studied and mingled with bright Hispanic officers from Latin America.

As far as growing up as a military brat, I will have to agree with my sister. I never felt that the traveling, meeting new friends, schools, or adventures were ever a negative; rather, it was another kind of school that helped teach me many things that have stuck with me through the years. I went to three high schools in three countries, which provided me the opportunity to see how lucky we are as Americans. I learned how fortunate we are to rely on police officers that we can trust, how easily we can jump in the car to go to the movies or get groceries, and how rare it is around the world to be able to act and speak freely.

Of the eighteen years that I lived with my parents and sister, what I remember most was the military way of life—we faithfully observed the wonderful holidays that make our nation great, we tried our best to be punctual for mass on Sundays and the other functions that we attended, and my family was the most important thing to me in the world. And even now that I am thirty-three years old and married, my family members are still my best friends and the only confidantes that I will ever need.

Moving all the time as a military brat, I did not get the opportunity to pick and choose my friends. Rather, I became friends with the first person to say hello to me or with the members of the athletic teams I tried out for. Eventually I met people who shared similar interests in music or sports or who sparked my interests intellectually, but race was the last thing on our minds. It was more about belonging to what eventually became our new military family.

My parents and my sister made me who I am today. My parents showed me what a family should be like. They valued respect, showed me how to overcome obstacles, taught me to smile through rough times, and most significantly, they showed me the importance of loving those around me. My sister showed me that a sibling can and should be a best friend while growing up. And now that I am married, my wife has become another addition to our tight-knit group, just as my brother-in-law has ever since we welcomed him to our family back in 2000.

We had our rough times as every family does, but overall, our household remained rich with happiness, love, and tradition. We all continue to hold the belief that family comes first. To this day, we eat dinner together as often as possible, play golf together, open presents on Christmas Eve, attend mass together, and value each other's company whenever and wherever possible. Not everyone has this while growing up, or even as an adult, so I understand how very fortunate I am. I was very lucky to receive the upbringing I did, and I cherish the values instilled in me by my family.

In various interviews shown in the media, Tiger Woods often speaks of his family's support and the fact that he never had to worry about failing. At a very young age, the support of his family pushed him to take chances, or at least try to attain his goals. Obviously this feeling of security within his family encouraged Tiger Woods to become the golfer and person he is today. My sister and I have always felt the same way. I knew that as I long as I tried my best, my family would support me regardless of the outcome. In a way, I had the security of knowing that I would always be a winner in their eyes.

"Is your dad retired yet, what's he doing now?" I hear this question about my father a lot these days, and I look forward to telling people what he's up to for many years to come.

CHAPTER 8

The Future of the Army: The Significance of Diversity

In wartime a man must do his duty as he sees it, and take his luck as it comes or goes.

—Winston Churchill

I constantly miss the twenty-one soldiers I buried, and I often wish that I could ascribe a higher purpose to their deaths. Did their deaths and the sacrifices of their families buy the rest of us time to enjoy the freedom that they fought to preserve? These soldiers continued to march despite having little more than an inkling of understanding of the fog of war and the toll it exacts on its participants and the heartbreak of being separated so long from their loved ones. But every Hispanic soldier marches on, further cementing the pride that their families and most Americans feel when they think of the sons and daughters who put everything on the line for our nation. For the most part, this sense of pride transcends politics and the personal beliefs we all have about the validity of the conflict. These soldiers do not allow the taste of chaos and the creeping desperation that accompanies the conflict to deter them from being recruited and reenlisted.

Whether the army knows it or not, they are engaged in a war for America's talent. Recruiting and retaining the right people has become increasingly difficult in the face of a competitive workforce and boundless opportunities for self-improvement through education. Our awesome army recruiters have literally become miracle workers, but they are often the first to admit that they stay awake at night wondering just how to persuade our youth to consider military service as a viable career option. If we are already having trouble retaining a professional military and inducing a good number of people to join the military, we had better develop a strategic plan to foster diversity within our corps with an eye to the future.

Hispanics will play a much bigger role in the military once the army figures out how important we are to its continued success. Once Hispanics as a demographic group become more educated and better equipped to engage in our increasingly complex high tech world, demand for Hispanics in all strata of the workforce will skyrocket. I predict that career decision-making will become an even greater challenge for Hispanics, thanks to the ever-changing pressures of global competition, workforce upheaval, and ongoing changes in our nation's policies toward immigration. Hispanics—so long as they place themselves in a good position to compete—face a bright future, because their increasing power and bilingual and multi-cultural roots will be too advantageous to ignore. It is up to the army to recognize these changes and make the appropriate institutional adjustments before it is too late.

The question we face now is whether we should recalibrate our forces to create a better understanding between the army and the Hispanic soldier or if we should instead allow this situation to lie dormant. I believe that our army should no longer adhere to the course of the past. Instead, we must work now to foster positive change for the army's—and the nation's—future.

We have very valuable soldiers who continue to be challenged by the rigors of war. The army is doing a magnificent job in training these soldiers and taking care of their families. I feel the need to assist in this process, because I have a vested interest in the success of our endeavor.

As some of this nation's earliest citizens, the Hispanic imprint on America's persona is indelible. The immigration debate has awakened a cultural war within the American psyche, but it is imperative that we do not allow the passions of our citizens to alienate the young Hispanic youth, who still see the army as an opportunity to contribute to the American legacy just like the generations of immigrant soldiers before them. At the risk of trotting out a well-worn cliché, I remind all Americans that our younger generation is our future. It is important that we honor the legacy of Hispanic Americans; after all, Hispanic culture is already deeply ingrained within America's borders, history, lifestyle, and military. If we allow the blood and sacrifice of yesterday's and today's Hispanic soldiers to be taken for granted, we risk turning away the next generation of Hispanic leaders.

Today, Hispanic servicemen and women epitomize everything that the army is and can be and what the nation needs most. As our country grows, it is incumbent on the military to set the stage for a strategic plan to foster diversity within the ranks. Many articles have appeared in the *Army Times* that examined the general officer numbers and the breakdown by gender and ethnicity. For example, as of December 31, 2005, of the 318 general officers in the army, only four of them were Hispanic.[8] Time and again, these articles express concerns about recruiting and promotion trends with blacks and Hispanics.

It is blindingly obvious that there is currently no explanation for the chasm between general officers and enlistment numbers and why this chasm inversely reflects our nation's current demographic trends. There is no explanation provided for the difficulties in transcending these problems. Many general officers believe that this issue falls into someone else's sandbox. If that is the case, who is supposed to grapple with this issue? Hispanics? Is this solely a Hispanic issue, and does the army believe that its diversity problems should be solved by Hispanics alone? If that is the army's belief, can Hispanics solve this problem while they are on active duty, or is the risk of alienating their peers too great for these Hispanic leaders? Remember, the army as an institution is always a bit confused in dealing with its members who do not toe the so-called "company line." Iconoclasts who oppose popular ideas, even those with good intentions, are often frustrated by institutional rigidity and resistance to criticism. What I am stating here is a gentle criticism of the army. I understand, as much as anyone, the importance of self-discipline and uniformity of opinion when necessary. But the military's values should not trump important questions that need to be asked in order to preserve the long-term viability of the army. Although change could be made, the U.S. Army's system for promotion is absolutely fair and honest. I sat on fifteen promotion boards and four command boards, and each one was unique in its own way. Yet all of them focused on providing the best officers and NCOs to lead our nation's soldiers.

A close and dear friend of mine for the past forty years—one who spent two tours in Vietnam as an enlisted soldier and as an officer—came to me recently and asked for my guidance and feedback in responding to a number of articles in the *Army Times* dealing with diversity. I will confess that I collaborated on the following letter to the editor in response to these articles. A shortened version appeared in the newspaper, but I am including the original, full letter that I wrote. I alone will assume responsibility for the final observations, as well as all procedural and substantive errors that may be contained within.

Dear Editor:

Diversity? In the U.S. Army? Who are we kidding?

I was absolutely appalled at the recent article in the *Army Times* that gave the statistics of each ethnicity group as it is represented in the senior flag ranks. Do these statistics also apply to senior level through junior level soldiers? More importantly, do they match the demographics of the United States? The army has been working on diversity for years, and it's even worse at the DOD level where the other services are just as bad but much better than in the army.

A much better statistical analysis would have been to compare the senior level to the enlisted ranks, by race, MOS, and the numbers killed, wounded, and decorated. I would venture to say that a much truer picture would have unfolded. In fact, my statistics show that if you just compare the number of Asian-Pacific generals per number of enlisted soldiers that are on active duty, you would have a very large disparity. An even more telling figure would be the number of African-America generals and the ratio of them to their combat arms soldiers in the corps/divisions, and the numbers of their casualties, wounded, and decorated; my thoughts are that you would be absolutely shocked.

Hispanic numbers at the general officer level is dismal compared to the number of Hispanic NCOs and soldiers in the ranks. And because of the large number of Hispanic soldiers in the Special Operations, Special Forces, Rangers, Infantry, Artillery, and Armor units, there is a much higher number of casualties among Hispanic soldiers. To compliment the aforementioned numbers, we have only fourteen female GOs and only one three-star. Forget the minority, and all the emphasis on recruiting leaves the honorable Hispanic soldier wandering why we are underrepresented at the higher levels. My guess is that although we have come a long way, we will do no better for the next 232 years, because the strategic plan on diversity is *all talk* and *no action*. But that's okay because it really starts with the president, his secretary of defense, and the problem is further exacerbated by the army. I am just glad we produce outstanding soldiers who are simply focused on serving this country and not on the numbers, as of yet. After all, they have been briefed that a diversity plan is forthcoming, but I wonder if it includes Hispanics?

I was briefed that the diversity plan was almost due thirty-six years ago, and I have been waiting ever since. I served two combat tours in Vietnam and have yet to see the difference. The first tour was as an enlisted soldier, and I saw many Hispanics. But for the second tour, I was a commissioned officer, and we were far and fewer in between. Ironically, I was selected in 1971 to visit the colleges and universities in the southwestern United States to recruit Hispanic college graduates in the U.S. Army to serve as commissioned officers and serve this country. I feel let down, because of all the Hispanics that have been recruited or enlisted in the army there are *so few Hispanics* at the general officer level. Thirty years later, I look around, check the statistics, and see more Hispanic soldiers and NCOs, but I just can't seem to see Hispanic battalion and brigade commanders, much less general officers. If you don't think our soldiers can see the total disparity in the number of Hispanic soldiers to general officer ratio, you are underestimating the pride and joy of great soldiers who have won forty Congressional Medals of Honor, not to mention four of whom were noncitizens at the time.

The Vietnam Wall depicts twenty-eight percent Hispanics, so if you say that education will deter enlistments, you are also looking at losing more combat soldiers in the force. Whereas the lack of education for Hispanics may be our demise to enlisting and staying in the army, you can not dismiss the fact that there are very few senior level role models, mentors, and overall cultural understanding.

So much for diversity.

Hispanic soldiers face four very important challenges in or out of the U.S. Army. Cultural differences, inadequate command of the English language, the lack of meaningful mentorship opportunities, and the lack of a solid educational foundation are all significant hurdles Hispanics must conquer before they can truly find success in life. The real question is whether Hispanics can compete at the highest levels, provided that they obtain a good education, learn to comprehend the institutional biases against cultural differences, immerse themselves in the English language, and receive help from the right mentors along the way. If these four components are the key to success for Hispanics in the army and in civilian life, why do

Hispanic success stories seem so rare? It is one thing to blame the military for our troubles, but the fact is that most Hispanic Americans sorely need to reevaluate their personal priorities. In order to persuade the army and other institutions to reevaluate their policies to help Hispanics succeed, we must come from a position of credibility in the way we approach our lives.

The dichotomy of both sides setting the tables for success is dependent on implementing a strategic plan that focuses on, and takes advantage of, our diversity. Without this plan, Hispanics are more likely to view the army's intentions with skepticism and cynicism. Worse, the army will find itself weakened as more Hispanics openly question the sincerity of the institution in its efforts to promote everyone fairly across the board. I'm not here to attack the present promotional system the army has in place, but I can't help but wonder how much more effective it would be if we had a plan in place to properly address issues of diversity. Perception is everything, and a strategic plan would dispel notions that the system is flawed, or even worse, rigged. Would this plan ultimately make a dent in the current diversity chasm? We'll never know until we take the time to implement a plan.

Not everyone has a vested interest in how our army demographically compares to the nation it protects, but it is important that this great military does everything in its power to promote fairness and diversity within its ranks. Although the implementation of a diversity plan is no panacea, and it guarantees no magic fix, ignoring the problem is potentially more damaging because it misleads our soldiers into thinking that their contributions are unimportant or unappreciated. After all, if we are truly committed to recruiting and retaining Hispanic soldiers like we have professed in the past with African-American soldiers, it isn't unfeasible to lay out the framework of a plan that properly acknowledges and rewards the contributions and talents of our Hispanic soldiers. All of this can be done in a way that honors real people, where we inject the personal into personnel and make it easy for all soldiers who fight for this country to have a seat at the table. General Douglas MacArthur drove this point home in his 1933 annual report to the Chief of Staff of the Army, arguing that "[t]he unfailing formula for production of morale is patriotism, self-respect, discipline, and self-confidence within a military unit, joined with fair treatment and merited appreciation from without...[morale] will quickly wither and die if soldiers come to believe themselves the victims of indifference or injustice on the part of their government, or of ignorance, personal ambition, or ineptitude on the part of their military leaders."[9] In other words, the army must never risk creating the perception that it doesn't value its soldiers and isn't willing to accommodate their most basic human needs.

Speaking of diversity, the institution needs to consider one other serious issue. Because we have a volunteer military force, soldiers have the right to elect their own ethnicity classification and may choose not to declare their ethnicity at all. At the same time, the institution may not be able to identify the ethnicity of surnames, and thus Hispanic soldiers could be classified as "white" (Anglo American) or "other." During my career, I was "other" for my first ten years of active duty and "white" for the next ten years. It wasn't until my final ten years of active duty that I was encouraged to check the Hispanic box. Today, we have a general with a Hispanic surname who chose not to declare his ethnicity and, therefore, isn't counted as part of our Hispanic general officer population. We also have wounded and dying soldiers who aren't counted as Hispanics because they either didn't want to be classified as such or because the U.S. Army didn't recognize the surname or failed to ask. David Cantu Bradley, for example, is a Congressional Medal of Honor recipient from Laredo, Texas, who chose not to use his Hispanic surname because he was afraid he wouldn't be sent to the front line. There are soldiers from the Philippines and Guam who also have Hispanic surnames but are categorized as "Asian Pacific Islanders." In the world of diversity and interracial marriages, surnames may not necessarily dictate the heritage of the soldier, and choosing which box to check is difficult at best. The bottom line is that as long as there is a choice, the institutional numbers of ethnicity breakdown will be skewed and deceiving. For census purposes, America and the U.S. Army need to get their arms around this sensitive and delicate problem, which currently borders on subtle discrimination. And as long as residents (noncitizens) can join the military, the institution, the country, and the general public need to recognize that this is not an issue of immigration reform but one of reexamining the military's current system of ethnicity classification.

Our enemies fear one thing most of all: a powerful nation made up of all ethnicities, faiths, genders, and types of people. No other country can pull off this undertaking. After all, we are the original "melting pot," and all types of people have come to this country because of its promise. Other countries know that the diversity that has been created by our American experiment makes us singularly special, and I believe that others are often envious of our resulting greatness. Successful institutions with smart business plans do not fail to consider diversity in their planning initiatives. They realize that the promotion of diversity results in a greater number of people finding hope in the American dream. Ultimately, the continuing hope and ambition of Hispanic Americans is the key to the army's continuing success. If this is true, then Hispanic generals with names such as Hernandez, Castro, Ramirez, Riojas, and Pagan can carry the banner forward knowing that colonels with names like Salazar, Riera, and Velez are right behind them, carrying that same torch of hope. We are in good hands, but the chosen few have much work to do if we are to continue to make strides in the ongoing transformation of this army.

As Hispanic Americans, we must also be honest and vigilant in considering our own collective weaknesses, both real and perceived. Our pride and our work ethic are sometimes misinterpreted as greed or blind ambition. And Hispanics often collectively splinter into countless numbers of subgroups, each zealously promoting its own agenda. When this splintering occurs, too often we find ourselves victimized by a circular firing squad that our dissension helped create. Those who oppose Hispanic progress delight in these occurrences, because we provide much of the ammunition for our downfall. To be clear, the diversity of those who call themselves Hispanic Americans sometimes demands more specialized representation; however, this representation need not come at the expense of our collective well-being. If you are white or black, you are just that. But Hispanics can be Cuban, Mexican, Puerto Rican, Central American, South American, of Portuguese descent (either Portugal or Brazil), Spanish or Black Hispanic. And this designation is made only if you take the time and trouble to declare it.

We must work to transcend the story of the fabled crabs (the theory of the crabs, *la teoria del cangrejo*) that jealously pull down their brethren to ensure that no one escapes the fisherman's bucket. Hispanic soldiers must strive to ensure that our best and brightest reach their full potential. In other words, we must all extend our hands to help the many ascending minority soldiers achieve—and exceed—their goals and dreams. We are all responsible for our social advancement, and no resource should be spared to ensure that our best soldiers eventually land among the stars.

In my thirty-three-year army career, I could not help but notice how certain soldiers are hailed as celebrities, at the same time that other soldiers are ignored. All too often, our society has been guilty of manufacturing heroes—only to discard them later when they are no longer needed. As we continue in this long and difficult war, I am convinced that we need to turn the lens inward on Americans as a reminder that not all heroism is absolute and not all enemies come from the outside. We must never allow the heroism of our soldiers to be an either/or proposition, nor should we allow them to be exploited by any party or movement for political gain.

In other words, here is our challenge: we must see talent, not skin color; we must follow spirituality, not celebrity; we must honor integrity, not self interest. If we as a nation begin to see the world, including ourselves, through this lens, then we can begin to truly understand the promise of our generation and our legacy to future generations.

EPILOGUE

CLOSING THOUGHTS ON OUR FALLEN SOLDIERS

History does not long entrust the care of freedom to the weak or the timid.

—General Dwight D. Eisenhower

None of the fallen soldiers whom I buried would have characterized themselves as true heroes; in fact, I doubt that the soldiers who lived or were injured would consider themselves that way either. They would emphatically say that they are just veterans who did what anyone else in their position would have done.

I, in turn, will accept hero status only after we all understand that Hispanic soldiers have been true heroes throughout our nation's history, and they have done it through 232 years of hard work and perseverance with little consideration given to fanfare or glory. I am a proud advocate for their legacy, and I am honored to be considered in the same light as these brave and selfless heroes. To share even a small part of their heroic lineage is simply the greatest honor I will ever know as a soldier.

Not everyone on the list I provided in the dedication considered themselves a hero based on their actions on the battlefield. In fact, many of them would be guilt-ridden from receiving special treatment or being labeled a hero. A few were cited for their courage in standing up for their principles, for the bravery they extended to their fellow soldiers, or for the standard they set every day of their lives. There are many, many individuals whom I have not named, who are an inspiration to our future generations and provide an emphatic answer to those who question the worth of this new generation of young men and women.

War provides countless examples of faceless heroism, of decorated veterans who don't want to remember and sometimes withdraw into themselves, refusing to revisit their exploits and even hiding their medals. This compassionate, cautionary tale hopefully speaks with eloquence about our modern armed forces, made up of the best and brightest young men and women who volunteered for the most demanding of calls and never wavered or turned away from what this nation asked of them. Our national identity currently stands at a crossroads; as all Americans debate the success of our War on Terror and the possibility of peace and true democratic reform in Iraq and Afghanistan, we need true uniformed heroes more than ever. But we need to accept these heroes on their terms. Our soldiers are not property to be exchanged for political capital, nor are they naïve children to be protected from danger and adversity. They are human beings who have courageously answered a call that most Americans have shied away from.

As I buried our fallen heroes, I wondered what it is that makes a soldier willing and able to charge into the face of the enemy while knowing that he is likely to die as a result. Perhaps a soldier's spirituality or passionate love of his country causes him to feel intoxicated by the thrill of victory while removing the masks of glory and valor. Or perhaps it is his human instinct that recognizes the need to give everything he has at the moment of truth. Maybe the truth is more complex, and a number of disparate circumstances tailored to the moment—such as accident, training, or even genuine love for another—give rise to that moment of "no greater love." These soldiers were compelled to remove the warrior's steely mask, stare destiny in the face without blinking, and ultimately greet their fate with love in their hearts. To me, this is what the phrase "no greater love" means to these fallen warriors.

The families of these Hispanic soldiers always impressed upon me that they were proud of the service of their husbands, wives, sons, and daughters, and this pride was heightened in light of the fact that they had selflessly laid down their lives for others. Many of these parents had intimated to me that they found solace in the unimpeachable character of their fallen children, especially when so many of their peers who stayed behind had succumbed to drug abuse, gangs, car accidents, or lives in which special and valuable talents went untapped. Of course, each family grieved in its own personal way, but I made it my job to remind them that their children had joined a long lineage of heroes who had given up everything to protect their brothers in arms and this country. These families were confused, dazed, lost, and many times new to the grieving process; however, none of the families I encountered ever expressed bitterness toward U.S. Army.

Of course, personal issues and feelings of anger would arise in the course of preparations for the memorial service. The flood of emotions that occurs whenever a cherished loved one is lost is common and inescapable; as a result, I found myself balancing the families' need for sympathy and respect with my personal and professional need to express gratitude for their personal sacrifice. The discussions I had with these families were often spirited, but they were also cathartic for all parties involved. I will never disclose the specifics of the emotional issues that sometimes arose, but I feel confident that, in each of these funerals, the army laid to rest a beloved family member and a valuable soldier, and the family left with a inextinguishable pride in the service and character of their son, daughter, sister, brother, husband, wife, mother, or father.

I came to know a diverse group of soldiers through the memories shared with me by their grieving, yet proud families. The diversity of this collection of fallen heroes is representative of the growing diversity of the American populace. That said, these soldiers were still not close to being a representative cross-section of America. This group consisted of five only sons, two only daughters, five non-American citizens, several married but most were single, predominantly Catholic, hailing largely from the South and representative of the idyllic "small-town USA." Despite these differences, and their divergence from the general population, this group of fallen soldiers came incredibly close to constituting as much of an American warrior caste as our nation would allow.

Most of these soldiers came from lower income families, but all of them had pride in bettering themselves. They took their service and responsibilities seriously, but if asked, they could have collectively belted out the songs of the 1980s and 1990s with the enthusiasm of a Grammy winner. They had all grown up in a time of rapid technological advancement, cutting their teeth on Nintendos, CD players, and personal computers, and they took advantage of the Internet to stay informed and keep in touch with their loved ones. Awed by the physical prowess of others, they invariably measured themselves by that yardstick. They also held risk takers and those who defied impossible odds to achieve their goals in high regard. People such as Pope John Paul II, resourceful NASA engineers, and gutsy high school football players—were seen as the greatest of heroes.

As the sobering melody of "Taps" played and the caskets lowered for each of these heroes, I found myself reflecting on their service and character in light of the new war we find ourselves in. An anonymous passage reminds us all that destiny "determines who walks into your life…it's up to you to decide who you let walk away, who you let stay, and who you refuse to let go." If anything, all of these amazing soldiers volunteered for the army, believed that they fought for a just and right cause, and if called, they would make their family proud—and that's exactly what they did. It's up to the rest of us to honor them for their contributions to our lives, and to never let go of their memory.

The Hispanic soldiers whom I had the honor of burying and memorializing were all beautiful, exceptional souls. None of them took themselves too seriously, but they took their roles in life very seriously. To all of them, failing to fulfill their commitment would be a personal affront, and the fear of failing motivated and resonated within each of them. In the end, their sacrifice is translated into freedom; indeed, that is their incalculable gift to the rest of us. The respect and honor they have brought unto the Hispanic community is but another part of the unpayable debt that they bestowed on the rest of us.

Unfortunately, the fact that we know so little about these heroes is the continuing tragedy that accompanies their legacy; that being said, I hope these words will reverse that drought. After all, Hispanics and Americans alike should be proud of the legacy of these soldiers. *No Greater Love* simply depicts that band of brothers who carry the burdens of freedom and the annals of history in the palms of their hands.

We simply cannot allow ourselves as a society to take for granted the bravery of these soldiers; their acts of heroism give true meaning to the very freedoms that define us. If we allow their courage to go unappreciated, then we truly have committed a regrettable act of sacrilege, and we are undeserving of their demonstration of no greater love.

I find myself asking whether our army and nation can survive another 232 years. We can thrive far beyond that, but we all must continue to play a personal role in the lives of others, accept change for the opportunities it presents, and fight for who we are as a nation. If we fail to do that, the sacrifices and toil of those who went before us will go ultimately unappreciated. Worst of all, our character and culture will suffer. America stands out as a beacon to the rest of the world, because we value, more than any other country, the contents of the human heart. Americans don't place a whole lot of currency in class or skin color; instead, the depth of a person's character determines her value and destiny. If we begin to surrender these values for self-indulgence and pursuits devoid of value, we risk destroying everything our ancestors created and preserved for us.

Carl Eller said in his induction speech to the Pro Football Hall of Fame in 2004 that "if the future of America is to be strong, you must be strong. You must hear the cries of our forefathers and pick up the fight that has helped to make this country great and helped make it what it is today." His words were geared toward young African-American men, but the bulk of his message is relevant to young Hispanics and all members of the next generation of young Americans. Eller reminded young people that the freedoms that they partake of today exist only because of the toil and sacrifices made by previous generations.

We must all pick up the fight for the future of our nation; as Eisenhower said above, preservation of freedom and liberty is not a job for the timid or weak. We must all have the courage and commitment to secure our prosperity. The soldiers I buried all possessed these attributes. That doesn't make them special, but it makes them unique. The simple truth is that we all possess the courage and commitment to control and shape our destiny. It's up to us to recognize that fact and act accordingly. These soldiers did just that, and so should we.

We have never apologized for being Hispanic, whether resident or citizen. We haven't apologized for who we are, and we sure as hell should not start now. To do so would betray the generous and inclusive spirit of this great nation. Past heroes, present warriors, and future Spartans—all of these groups form the prestigious ranks of Hispanic heroes. While others armchair quarterback every aspect of the war, soldiers—and Hispanics especially—know their place in the scheme of things. Where too many others see the world through the myopic measuring sticks of days, weeks, and months, I believe that our soldiers realize that the true impact of their work will be judged by a dimension of decades, generations, even centuries.

Hispanics, whether or not they are residents or citizens, and whether they are Puerto Rican, Cuban, Mexican, Spanish, Central American, or South American, have put their lives on the line for their nation and/or adopted country. Without fanfare they just seem to be around when you need them most. Their love of country has motivated them to serve, and despite the odds, their ethnicity has never stopped their service to this country. I seriously doubt it ever will.

We must remember that immigration reform may have its place in today's world, but it must be exclusive of the armed forces. Otherwise, the rules drawn up years ago that have permitted residents and noncitizens to join the military and to play a role in fighting for our freedom will have been for naught. An ungrateful and un-American attitude would not benefit our country at this critical juncture in society, and we should not tolerate it. Standing up for these heroes during their journey to succeed is crucial and is what we as Americans are all about. After all, these Hispanic-American soldiers have been filled with high expectations, all the while knowing their dream would face failure, betrayal, and possible rejection. Yet their reward might just be the pride and satisfaction that come with being part of this country's future.

Hispanic-American soldiers, in their heroism and humility, epitomize nobility of service to country and, as Apostle John articulated, service above self. In giving up their lives, they entered the pantheon of the greatest American heroes, showing their brothers-in-arms and their nation the immeasurable depth of the heart of one who chooses to sacrifice everything for another. Thus, these souls have become immortal representatives of today's American character, and they symbolize the real spirit to help and defend.

While others debate the events of yesterday and today, our Hispanic soldiers make history and change lives for the future. After all, Hispanics have done things the old-fashioned way throughout American history, with integrity, humility, and hard work. While naysayers question their commitment and loyalty, Hispanic Americans have worked tirelessly to contribute to the greatness of our nation. Apostle John meant what he said in chapter 15:13. Any one of us may be called on to give everything we have for another, and that's exactly what the twenty-one men and women I buried did. The least we can do now is honor these heroes in our prayers and the sweet memories they left behind. Failure to do that is not just ungrateful, it's un-American.

NOTES

[1] U.S. Department of Defense, directive no. 1300.l5 (January 11, 2001): 2.

[2] U.S. Department of Defense (see endnote 1).

[3] Samuel H. Preston and Emily Buzzell, "Service in Iraq: Just How Risky?" *Washington Post*, August 26, 2006.

[4] Ernesto Uribe, "Are Hispanics the First to Fight, Last to be Promoted?" *Armed Forces J. International* 128 (January 1991): 42, 43.

[5] Samuel P. Huntington, *The Soldier and the State: The Theory and Politics of Civil-Military Relations* (Cambridge, MA: Belknap Press, 2005).

[6] Morris Janowitz, *The Professional Soldier* (Northampton, MA: Free Press, 1971).

[7] David W. Moore and B. Thomas Trout, "Military Advancement : The Visibility Theory of Promotion," *American Political Science Review* 72 (1978): 452–468.

[8] Gordon Lubold, "More minority officers needed, Rumsfeld says," *Army Times*, March 6, 2006.

[9] General Douglas MacArthur, annual report prepared for Chief of Staff of the Army, 1933.

ABOUT THE AUTHOR

MAJOR GENERAL FREDDIE VALENZUELA served thirty-three years in the U.S. Army and was highly decorated for heroism and valor. He served in three corps and six divisions all over the world, including Peru, Korea, Colombia, Turkey, Haiti, Kuwait, Grenada, Panama, Germany, El Salvador, and Somalia. He commanded in the Cold War and Gulf War eras, and he was awarded the Defense and Army Distinguished Service Medal.

After retirement, he created an educational foundation for at-risk children and for families of soldiers killed in the line of duty. He now sits on the community boards for the Boy Scouts, the Boys and Girls Club, and the Eagle Scout Foundation. He is an Eagle Scout himself and was inducted into the Boys and Girls Club Hall of Fame. He also sits on the national boards for St. Mary's University, Armor Designs, the Tomas Rivera Policy Institute, and USAA Federal Savings Bank. In addition, he is a senior consultant to the Center on Terrorism Law at St. Mary's University School of Law, where he was recently named a Distinguished Alumnus. As the president and CEO of three international business companies, he was named one of the most influential Hispanic Americans in the U.S. by *Hispanic Business* magazine.